VOICES OF INUIT LEADERSHIP AND
SELF-DETERMINATION IN CANADA

VOICES OF INUIT LEADERSHIP AND SELF-DETERMINATION IN CANADA

EDITED BY DAVID LOUGH

ISER Books

© 2020 David Lough

LIBRARY AND ARCHIVES CANADA CATALOGUING IN PUBLICATION
Title: Voices of Inuit leadership and self-determination in Canada / edited by David Lough.
Names: Lough, David, 1947- editor.
Series: Social and economic papers ; no. 37.
Description: Series statement: Social and economic papers ; 37 | Chapters inspired by a conference, the 2016 Inuit Studies Conference, held in St. John's, Newfoundland and Labrador. | Includes bibliographical references and index.
Identifiers: Canadiana (print) 20200240110 | Canadiana (ebook) 2020024020X | ISBN 9781894725699 (softcover) | ISBN 9781894725705 (PDF) | ISBN 9781894725712 (HTML) | ISBN 9781894725729 (Kindle)
Subjects: LCSH: Inuit—Canada. | LCSH: Leadership—Canada. | LCSH: Community leadership—Canada. |LCSH: Inuit—Canada—Politics and government. | CSH: Native leaders—Canada.
Classification: LCC HM781 .V65 2020 | DDC 303.3/40899712071—dc23

Cover photograph: © Eldred Allen (grasswork basket by Naomi Williams)
Cover design: Alison Carr
Page design and typesetting: Alison Carr
Copy editing: Iona Bulgin

Published by ISER Books
Institute of Social and Economic Research
Memorial University of Newfoundland
PO Box 4200
St. John's, NL A1C 5S7
www.hss.mun.ca/iserbooks/

Printed in Canada
26 25 24 23 22 21 20   1 2 3 4 5 6 7 8

Contents

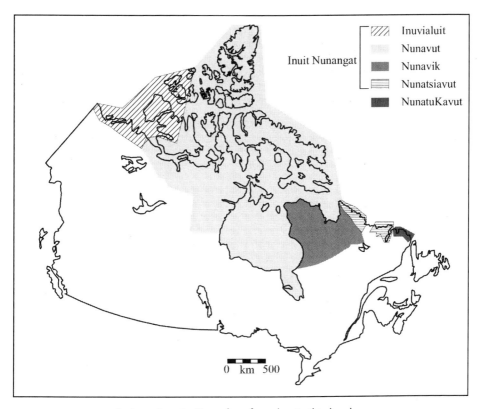

Inuit regions in Canada referred to in this book.

Acknowledgements

This volume is an outcome of the 20th Biennial Inuit Studies Conference, hosted in St. John's, Newfoundland and Labrador, by the Nunatsiavut Government and Memorial University. The conference and all the publications which resulted from it were made possible by the generous financial and logistical support of the Nunatsiavut Government Department of Culture, Tourism and Recreation and several federal agencies including the Department of Indigenous and Northern Affairs (INAC), the Department of Canadian Heritage (PCH), and Parks Canada.

For its part, Memorial supported the conference through financial contributions from its research, teaching, and engagement programs. The Tradition and Transition Partnership, administered by MUN, made further financial contributions, generously supplemented by a SSHRC Connections Grant to cover costs associated with keynote and international speakers.

Chapters that began as keynote addresses and panel discussions were transcribed by student research assistant Michelle Saunders. The publication of this volume would not have been possible without the generous and valuable editorial assistance provided by Dr. Peter Ramsden. We are also grateful for the encouragement and support of ISER Books and, in particular, its academic editor, Dr. Fiona Polack.

Introduction

Tom Gordon, David Lough, and Lisa Rankin

In 2015 the Nunatsiavut Government and Memorial University of Newfoundland were awarded a five-year SSHRC Partnership Grant, Tradition and Transition among the Labrador Inuit. The central tenet of the partnership was to provide a respectful forum from which to co-create and share Inuit and academic knowledge deemed beneficial to Inuit self-governance. Following lengthy community consultations, leadership emerged as a primary theme to be addressed by the partnership. From the fifteenth century to achieving self-government in 2005, Labrador Inuit have lived and expressed traditions of leadership passed between generations and across a history of engagement with other Indigenous peoples, transient Europeans, and ultimately settlers. Though well documented, this history had been less than fully considered, but as Nunatsiavut moves forward from its birth as a political entity to a mature expression of a contemporary Indigenous society, the Inuit of Labrador hope to develop a profound understanding of how cultural traditions could guide them into that future.

The Tradition and Transition Research Partnership has focused on past, current, and future leadership in order to understand the context and development of Labrador Inuit cultural identity for the purpose of strengthening Indigenous self-governance. Comparisons with other Inuit governments across the Nunangat are central to this work, but so too is understanding leadership from multiple perspectives. Honouring the diversity of Inuit experience across the continua of gender and age has therefore been an essential component of the partnership's methodology. More important, however, was creating accessible and culturally appropriate spaces and formats to share this knowledge. The 2016 Inuit Studies Conference, hosted by the partnership, was the first venue to put these goals to the test, allowing Tradition and Transition members to communicate research results alongside invited keynote addresses delivered by contemporary Inuit leaders, and panel sessions organized by Inuit across the Nunangat and beyond. The timeliness of our own explorations of questions around Inuit leadership was confirmed by the quantity and quality of the conference presentations.

The current volume is a collection of reflections on Inuit leadership stimulated by this conference and edited for publication by the authors in the ensuing months. What is compelling here is the broad range of perspectives brought to bear on the topic. This anthology joins voices that come from deep within Inuit society with voices that offer the perspective of external observation. These voices speak in future, present, and past tenses. From current visions of what Inuit leadership is and future challenges to the social and historical precedents which shaped it, a composite vision emerges: a vision which speaks to the meaning of Inuit leadership in twenty-first-century Canada. These perspectives converge in a pattern of complementation rather than opposition, a layering of different ways of seeing and knowing that enrich understanding as they bump into and complete one another and interlock. The very diversity of voices heard here becomes the strength of the whole as a composite picture of Inuit leadership grows.

These are the voices of both Inuit and non-Inuit, united in their commitment to understanding what Inuit leadership is, has been, and will be. Among the Inuit voices are those of leaders themselves, both present and future. We also hear from Inuit witnesses to leadership: knowledge-bearers, community stewards, questioners, activists, and observant individuals. The non-Inuit voices include academic researchers who have observed and analyzed Inuit leadership across decades and non-Inuit knowledge-workers who have spent careers working in the north, assisting in the development of social and political structures in which Inuit leadership has prospered.

But the multivocality represented here is not a simple binary division between Indigenous and non-Indigenous contributors. Inuit Nunangat has one of the youngest populations in the world. At the same time, Inuit culture places its deepest confidence in Elder knowledge. Thus, it has been critical that the voices heard here counterpoint the aspirations of youth with the wise counsel of Elders. The visions of leadership cast here reflect these perspectives well, not only in the balance of experience lived with experience anticipated but in the respect that flows across these generations.

Also represented here is a dialogue between the perspectives on leadership rooted in lived experience and those developed from observations with an outsider's perspective. These perspectives balance first- and third-person reflections, bringing with them the deep involvement inherent in the former with the objectivity essential to the latter.

The forms that these voices chose to communicate offer perhaps the most insightful complementation. Standard academic publications often suppress Indigenous knowledge, forcing observations into western frameworks. Therefore, we have chosen to allow multiple formats in this volume, preserving the diversity of knowledge and backgrounds, while making the volume accessible to a wide variety of readers. Several of the Inuit contributors have chosen the medium of storytelling to provide an understanding of what Inuit leadership is. Narratives around exemplary leadership, personal vignettes, and the expression of ambitious dreams align with the traditions of Inuit storytelling. These told narratives retain a conversational voice, inviting the reader into shared confidences and aspirations. Other contributors communicate through the structured dialectic of critical discourse, assembling evidence and arguing it to a conclusion. It is along the continuum that links these two distant modes of communication that the most nuanced understandings of Inuit leadership can be found.

Equally as wide as the range of voices heard in this volume are the platforms on which Inuit leadership is exercised. While pride of place obviously falls to the political sphere, this arena for Inuit leadership which has created the movement toward self-determination is not the only form of leadership examined in these chapters. The future of Inuit Nunangat is dependent not only on strong and courageous political leadership rooted in Inuit traditions and cultural values but, equally, it will require Inuit control of the knowledge creation which will guide it with integrity through that future. Thus, while a considerable number of the chapters deal with the roots of and routes to Inuit self-determination in the political sphere, others consider the critical role that Inuit must play in establishing and controlling research agendas. In contrast to the past, where Inuit studies have been conceived and conducted largely by academic researchers from the south, recent and future practice has shifted research orientations to the expressed needs of Inuit Nunangat. Inuit have begun, and must continue, to assume full responsibility for determining and directing the research agendas based on community priorities. Research in and for Inuit Nunangat must rely on full participation of Inuit researchers and knowledge-bearers. New ways of blending traditional knowledge with scientific methods of creating knowledge have to be forged. Accelerated opportunities for research training for Inuit need to be mandated both within the north and with partner institutions in the south. Examples of the challenges to and the essential benefits of Inuit leadership in research in the north are found in several chapters.

A further forum for understanding Inuit leadership is the cultural narrative. The stories that illustrate Inuit leadership are being re-framed to reflect the unique forms and platforms for leadership in Inuit society. Their voices reveal Inuit values, values that define leadership on a scale that reflects the social conditions, community, and the physical environment shared across Inuit Nunangat. Among these are modes of leadership that are also expressions of gender. In traditional Inuit society, female and male responsibilities were diverse and complemented one another to assure the well-being of nuclear and extended families. In this context the ways in which Inuit women construct and demonstrate leadership is drawn from a distinct history of experience. Inuit women's approaches to leadership are articulated in this anthology through the voices of Inuit women leaders and researchers, as well as in the oral histories of women from across Nunatsiavut reflecting on the role models who shaped their own understanding of leadership and the ways in which that leadership is manifest in their communities.

To address questions of leadership directly, the conference organizers invited two contemporary Canadian Inuit leaders to share their visions in keynote addresses. Natan Obed's "The Path to Self-Determination" looks more to the future than the past as it charts a vision for Inuit autonomous governance in the twenty-first century. Obed challenges Inuit and Canadians alike to move beyond the settling and implementation of land claims to redefining the relationship between the Government of Canada and the Inuit as a self-determining people. A change is needed in the balance of power in defining control of policy and resources that affect the Inuit in the seven areas that are articulated in Inuit Tapiriit Kanatami's (ITK) Strategy and Action Plan. These range from suicide prevention to the environment, to curriculum to housing, to health and wellness. In striking that new balance, Obed repeats the refrain that reconciliation must move beyond talk to action and that action must engage and respect Inuit in every aspect of decision making. As he summarizes, "The way in which everyone—all Canadians—can play a role in Inuit self-determination is to accept that we have things to say, and that we do it in a way that respects our people and also respects human knowledge" (34).

While Obed's keynote set its sights squarely on the future, the president of the National Inuit Youth Council started her keynote address with a reflective gaze toward the past. Maatalii Okalik remembered the leadership models cast by earlier generations of Inuit who laid the groundwork for the youth of her generation. She showed a 1970s video clip of Inuk land claims negotiator John Amagoalik explaining Inuit aspirations to the panelists on the TV news quiz *Front Page Challenge*. Then as now, the future for Inuit lay in vesting power in the communities. The aspirations of today's Inuit youth include strengthening their relationship to their language, culture, and cultural practices. Pride in and the practice of culture are the keys to combatting the problems that plague these youth: suicide, educational deficits, and social disenfranchisement. Inuit youth need a knowledge of the catastrophes in recent history in order to reclaim pride in pre-colonial Inuit culture, a culture at risk of being lost. Initiatives that strengthen language and culture, implement an effective suicide prevention strategy, address social inequities, and encourage empowerment through education reflective of Inuit values are the necessary steps to true and meaningful reconciliation.

The social and cultural determinants of leadership and governance are explored through close lenses in the collaborative project *Daughters of Mikak: Celebrating Inuit Women's Leadership in Nunatsiavut*. In *Daughters of Mikak*, a digital library of oral history, Inuit women of all generations across Nunatsiavut narrated the stories of the women who had shaped them. From these stories, Beverly Hunter, an addictions and trauma counsellor with Nunatsiavut's Department of Health and Social Development; Charlotte Wolfrey, AngajukKâk of Rigolet and an advocate against family violence; and Andrea Procter, social justice researcher and an adjunct professor in Memorial University's Department of Gender Studies, have extrapolated profiles of Inuit women's leadership in "Inuit Women's Leadership: A Nunatsiavut-Based Narrative." This chapter's chorus of Inuit voices illustrates and honours the distinct leadership style of women in Nunatsiavut who created social networks that have withstood the impacts of colonialism.

David Lough charts a parallel trajectory for Nunatsiavut as a whole, focusing particularly on the qualities of leadership demonstrated by the architects of Nunatsiavut, in "Labrador Inuit Leadership—1970s to 2005." Formerly deputy minister of Culture, Recreation and Tourism in the Nunatsiavut Government, Lough worked in various capacities with Labrador Inuit leaders across four decades. While the Nunatsiavut Government is a young political entity, it was born out of more than thirty years of reflection and negotiation on social authority and mediated political culture. That gestation was informed by more than 250 years of simultaneous resistance, negotiation, and empowerment between the Labrador Inuit and European/southern colonial powers. Lough offers an informed and personal observation on Nunatsiavut's march toward self-determination.

Two chapters relate the evolution of Inuit self-governance in Canada in the first decades of the twenty-first century and offer

preliminary assessments of the effectiveness of the institutions which
have emerged and the accomplishments of the individuals who have
led them. Bruce Uviluq, a negotiator with the Legal Services Division
at Nunavut Tunngavik Incorporated (NTI), examines the creation of
the territory of Nunavut in "The Nunavut Land Claims Agreement:
A Modern Treaty." Modern treaties with Indigenous peoples, like
Nunavut's 1993 land claims agreement with Canada, share one
theme: resources. Uviluq premises his discussion on the "hard
truth ... that if the resources were not on Indigenous peoples' lands,
we probably would not have treaties today" (117). Uviluq surveys the
comprehensive land claims settlements in Canada since 1975, leading to the Nunavut Land Claims Agreement (NLCA), signed in 1993
after seventeen years of negotiations and creating the Territory and
Government of Nunavut. The NLCA established innovative governing structures to facilitate co-management of resources and to assure
that benefits would return to Inuit. However clear these frameworks,
the implementation has not been without complications, largely
rooted in cultural differences in understanding the frameworks.
While the Inuit regarded them as the bases for discussions, the federal government saw them as a *fait accompli*. A 2016 lawsuit by the
NTI representing the Inuit of Nunavut against the federal government for NLCA non-compliance was settled in favour of the Inuit
with a cash settlement and a markedly improved process for treaty
implementation.

To add analysis to the narrative of the path to political autonomy,
political scientists Graham White and Christopher Alcantara draw
insightful comparisons between the two jurisdictions in "Institutional
Design and Inuit Governance: Nunatsiavut and Nunavut Compared."
Both White, an emeritus professor of Political Science at the University of Toronto, and Alcantara, an associate professor of Political

Science at the University of Western Ontario, have published extensively on governance and intergovernmental co-operation between Indigenous and non-Indigenous communities in Canada. Their detailed comparison of Inuit governance in Nunatsiavut and Nunavut examines the differences and similarities in categories of representation and participation between the self-government of the Labrador Inuit as an autonomous Inuit region within a province and the "public" government of Nunavut, a territory with responsibility for Inuit and non-Indigenous citizens. Though many commonalities can be cited in the goals and aspirations to promoting Inuit representation, inclusiveness, responsiveness, and participation, stark contrasts between these two Inuit jurisdictions have resulted from fundamental differences in governance structures and practices; in the historical context of land claims negotiation; in the size, makeup, and geographic distribution of populations; and in the relationships to other levels of government. While White and Alcantara pass no judgment on these differences, their comparisons offer analysis which may "help Inuit better understand the effects of their institutional design choices and whether reforms are needed to achieve the priorities of their residents, beneficiaries, and political leaders" (126).

Self-determination necessitates agency in knowledge creation. The relationship between research agency and political autonomy is made explicit in Amy Hudson and Julie Bull's "Reclaiming Inuit Knowledge in Pursuit of Self-Governance: Regulating Research through Relationships." Both authors have been engaged with research governance in the southern Inuit communities of NunatuKavut in central and coastal Labrador. Amy Hudson, manager of Research, Education and Culture at the NunatuKavut Community Council (NCC), is a PhD candidate at Memorial University specializing in Inuit community governance, self-determination, and sustainability.

Julie Bull, who holds a PhD in Indigenous research ethics, has more than fifteen years of experience in community-based research and education with Indigenous communities and is currently a Research Methods Specialist at the Centre for Addiction and Mental Health (CAMH). Projects undertaken in three pilot communities, together with a vast literature on Indigenous-led research, have brought them to an understanding of how Inuit autonomy in research both influences and creates pathways for Inuit self-determination. Further, they demonstrate how research grounded in relationships based on respect and reciprocity further enhance community capacity and outcomes by building on the strengths, expertise, and local knowledge of Inuit in their time and place.

Inuit agency in setting, directing, and fully participating in the research agenda is vital to the future of Inuit autonomy. Several conference presentations narrated the successes and lessons of community-driven, Inuit-led research projects from across the circumpolar north. From community monitoring initiatives to best practices in research training in the north, the recurrent theme focused on research autonomy by and for Inuit. One of the more interesting presentations was a roundtable organized by the Inuit Qaujisarvingat—the Inuit Knowledge Centre at ITK. Transcribed and annotated as "Strengthening Inuit Self-Determination in Research: Perspectives from Inuit Nunangat," the roundtable was anchored on presentations by representatives of the research agencies from regions of Inuit Nunangat. Moderated by ITK president Natan Obed, the roundtable's host, Inuit Qaujisarvingat, was represented by Scot Nickels, ITK's Special Advisor on Monitoring, Evaluation, and Learning. Nickels opened the discussion with an overview of ITK's Inuit Research Strategy. With a mandate of achieving Inuit self-determination in research, the strategy's objectives include developing Inuit-specific research priorities and methodologies, assuring research training for Inuit that values traditional knowledge, and establishing standards of research ethics and intellectual property rights that safeguard Inuit rights in research.

Ellen Avard is director of the Nunavik Research Centre (NRC), Makivik Corporation. Created in 1978 following the signing of the James Bay and Northern Quebec Agreement (JBNQA) to respond to Inuit research questions, the NRC is the oldest Inuit research organization in Canada. Avard provided an overview of five current research projects that demonstrate research activity that support wildlife management and country food security. Jennifer Parrott, research manager for the Inuvialuit Regional Corporation, outlined the provisions in the Inuvialuit Final Agreement that ensure the Inuit voice in all matters concerning renewable and non-renewable resources, as well as research. Collaborative research is protected by a research licencing process that requires direct involvement with local Inuvialuit organizations. The roundtable concluded with an animated Q & A session that expanded on the essentiality of Inuit self-determination in research.

Across the pages that follow a portrait of Inuit leadership for the twenty-first century emerges. It is both visionary and consensual, brutally honest about the past and optimistic for the future, respectful, and resilient. It is rooted in ancient cultural traditions, yet focused on a future that will define its political and cultural autonomy on the very principles that underscore that culture. It is determined in its will toward self-determination and resolute in its desire to assume control for the creation of knowledge about itself and its people.

PART I: LEADERSHIP

The Path to Self-Determination*

Natan Obed

I want to talk today about the path to self-determination. It's a path that we take every single day as Inuit. As I look around the room and reflect on those I've seen since I've been here this morning, I've seen a host of people that I've shared this path with, Inuit and non-Inuit alike. I've worked on Inuit issues now for fifteen years and, over that time, we have seen some significant changes—and we should be proud of them—but there still is much work to be done. The more that we get into the work, the more that we realize that sometimes we were not thinking of things in the right way, or that we were thinking in an incomplete set of circumstances about the problems that we were trying to solve.

I'll start today by talking a bit about cultural appropriation. Alethea Arnaquq-Baril [an Inuit filmmaker and activist, based in Iqaluit; owner of Unikkaat Studios production company] put up a Facebook post about five or six days ago about the Duchess of Cambridge, Kate Middleton, who, during her trip to Canada, was wearing ulu earrings that weren't made by an Inuk artist. Alethea talked about cultural

---

*   Editor's Note: This chapter is based on a transcript of Natan Obed's talk as it was delivered at the Inuit Studies Conference on October 8, 2016. It has been edited for readability, but otherwise it has been left largely in the format of an oral presentation.

appropriation and the meaning behind why this was something that we should consider as Canadians or artists or business people, and the context of what it means for Inuit to not own something that is yours and a symbol of your culture and society. Patent lawyers reading or hearing this are probably immediately thinking, "well under Canadian law this isn't an individual's item to hold"; you immediately start thinking about the reasons why Inuit can't say that we have any right to be able to exclusively make things that look like ulus. But you have to unpack this—you have to think about where we started, about the beginning of the land claims movement.

Inuit had to understand that the land that we had lived on and occupied since time immemorial wasn't actually ours: that the title that we had to it, that was tenuous at best, was called "Aboriginal title," and it's not simple in the way that you think of owning a home or a parcel of land. We had to explain our land use and occupancy to the Government of Canada just to be able to sit down and talk about a negotiation that would then lead to land claims agreements. So we were told that the land that was ours was actually not ours. Then you talk about, say, the minerals that are under our lands, or any of the natural resources that are under our lands: that those aren't ours either, and why—because subsurface is different than surface. I understand the Canadian constructs that govern us: the legislation, the Supreme Court rulings, the way in which the Canadian government has articulated this issue to Inuit. But again and again we see mining companies, we see natural resource developers, who come into our lands, and we negotiate with them for impact benefit agreements: we may get shared royalties with the province or territory in which we live; we may get business opportunities, if we meet the criteria that are set out as being "fair." But it comes back to the same issue: what we thought was ours isn't actually ours; and people can come onto our lands, and take from our lands, and leave us still a marginalized people and largely in poverty, while the wealth that is generated from those lands goes to private corporations and to the rest of Canada.

And then we have education—and actually this one hits home to just about everyone reading or listening to this. The way in which we educated our children, and the way in which we imagined them to be productive members of our society, was irrelevant: we were doing it the wrong way, and especially in the 1950s and 60s the idea was that Inuit needed to be put in residential schools and needed to be indoctrinated into a western construct, and not keep our language or our cultural ties or our ties to our parents, as a prerequisite for Inuit to be rehabilitated into "good Canadian citizens." The effects of that time still resonate today, so that we have an education system that still tells us "the way you educate your children is wrong, and you have to educate your children in a southern Canadian way."

And then we get into governance, the mobilization of Indigenous peoples in Canada, and the creation of Inuit Tapiriit Kanatami [ITK] in 1971. This was the driving force of Inuit representational organizations in settling land claims and restructuring the Canadian map—and that's exciting. But here we are in 2016, and when we say Indigenous peoples and Inuit need to have a participatory role in the way the government conducts its business, which is supported by the constitution and by the United Nations Declaration on the Rights of Indigenous Peoples, we are shown again and again that that request, and that reality, isn't taken seriously. So even the place that we occupy in Canada—the governance model that we've created, how we've self-determined to the world that this is who we are—can be overturned by a government bureaucrat who decides that they don't necessarily like Inuit Tapiriit Kanatami's position on things, so perhaps they'll bring in another individual Inuk, and who will represent the

Inuit voice differently. It could be something as small as cross-cultural training, or it could be something as large as consultation on particular program reviews. The fact remains that there is still a basic lack of respect for Inuit and the way in which we are trying to self-determine to the world.

So, to get back to the earrings. All of what I've said is behind Alethea's statement about earrings: that somehow no matter where we go, and no matter what we do, we are being told that who we are is secondary to who others want us to be, and our place in Canada is largely dictated by rules that we didn't create and governments see us more as adversaries than as equals or partners. So this is an example of how it then mushrooms out into the rest of society, where others take our cultural imagery and repurpose it and use it as their own, on their own terms, and describe to the world in a different way who we are, what we look like, how we dress, what items we use for daily life. I think that is at the heart of a lot of this frustration, and so here we are today talking about self-determination across a number of different cross-cutting issues, but I'll start with governance.

Inuit Tapiriit Kanatami is a democratic institution, and it doesn't need to exist. If you think about the role that we play, we only play a role because the four Inuit land claims regions have given us that role; the four presidents of our land claims organizations—the Nunatsiavut Government, Makivik Corporation, Inuvialuit Regional Corporation, and Nunavut Tunngavik Incorporated [NTI]—are our board of directors, and they elect the president of the organization and they direct the organization's mandate and its work. So it is a true expression of democracy, of Inuit democracy: every single one of you who is a beneficiary of one of our four land claims gets to elect your land claims organizational president, or your chair, in the case of the Inuvialuit Regional Corporation, and then those leaders, in considering of your interests, elect a national and international leader to represent Canadian Inuit. I don't have the power to do the things that I'm doing or say the things that I'm saying by myself; I didn't go and create a platform and a mandate for myself and then through lobbying and through public support get to where I am today. I am an agent of Inuit Tapiriit Kanatami. I'm an agent of the board. I am saying what they want me to say; my power comes from the regions, and I think that's really powerful, because not all Indigenous peoples have that luxury in Canada of being united enough to have a national president. This is really important, because all of the different constructs that we'll talk about today—the UN Declaration on the Rights of Indigenous Peoples, the overarching relationship between the Government of Canada and Inuit—that is all predicated on the idea that the Inuit counterpart of the Government of Canada is Inuit Tapiriit Kanatami, and we have decided that, and that's an exciting thing that is a step on the path to self-determination.

I want to talk a little bit about dreams and who gets to have them. I recently watched a Stephen Hawking movie. *The Theory of Everything* I think is the name, and it's interesting to me that a lot of his life work, even though he is renowned as one of the smartest people alive, was actually wrong—or more respectfully "has been debunked"— and he's moved on from his original constructs around black holes. That's interesting to me because entire societies believed what he had to say, entire groups of academics; it was so powerful to them and meant so much to them and it made so much sense that they followed that line of thinking for some time. Now, how that relates to us here today is in regard to who gets to decide what is best for us. So if you think about education, and how our children go to school, and what curriculum they use, what language they speak, whose bright idea is it? Or is it just a century and a half of principles that have been developed over time by Canada that then are just thrust upon Inuit, as if we can benefit from them the same way as somebody in suburban Ontario? Also the ideas about who we are in relation to Canada: when we dream of our place within Canada, I don't think I need a lawyer to do that; I don't think Inuit need lawyers to do that. Now, the legal construct is what we live in, and our ability to interact with legislation and policy is essential to our success as advocates for Inuit at ITK. But if you get down to the central tenet, the central questions, and you dream about a universe, you dream about the way the universe fits, and if you think about it as an Inuit universe, you go back to this idea of Aboriginal title, or go back to this idea of limitations on funding being the only things that are holding us back from achieving social equity, then you start to be able to open your thinking to what's possible. There's a health accord that's being negotiated right now between the federal government, the provinces, and the territories: why couldn't there be an Inuit health accord that puts the necessary funding forward to address some of our massive needs, especially in relation to mental health? It's entirely possible, but why would we not think that way? Because the federal government has already decided what the priorities are, and they've already entered into discussion with provinces and territories, who are service delivery agents, about how the federal ideas would be then implemented in provinces and territories. We also think about our policy space—what space do we occupy as Inuit?—and we'd like to say we occupy an Inuit Nunangat space: 35 per cent of Canada's land mass and 50 per cent of its coastline. The foundation for Arctic sovereignty: that's the space we say we occupy. But the federal government often thinks of this space as northern equals territorial, and other Inuit regions as falling outside a lot of those policy discussions. So even the ability to dream of the way in which the country works on Arctic issues is something that we don't have the right to control, but that doesn't mean that that can't happen. People in [the] dominant society can convince entire societies to believe in bad and incorrect ideas—it happens all the time—so the idea that what grounds us in our current realities is infallible, I reject. Likewise, the idea that we can't create a better pedagogy for education: I believe we can. Shouldn't it be based on what we want our Inuit children to become? Should we not be talking to academic institutions about what it means for the Inuit reality when an Alberta-based curriculum is the standard, because of the entrance requirements of colleges and universities, when so few of our students can go to those universities and colleges anyway without upgrading and years of struggle to get through?

The purpose of all of this, the purpose of the Inuit movement, land claims and otherwise, can get bigger and it can occupy larger spaces than we have already occupied and that's why I said that in my speech in Cambridge Bay last year, when I was in the election process. I would think that with all of the assets we have today—the fact that there are so many Inuit that are educated or that are knowledgeable and have wisdom, who are willing to work on the causes that we have been working on for forty or fifty years—there's no reason to think that we cannot make as big a difference today and tomorrow as our parents did creating land claims and creating representational organizations. I have a picture on my phone that I'm going to show the prime minister: it's of my father standing in what looks to be a parliamentary room, but standing with Pierre Trudeau and a couple of other Inuit leaders, and I want to show the prime minister this picture and talk about what it means to both of us to be sort of legacy children, where our parents worked on these issues and now we are working on them. But I also want to talk about how little has changed since then and the inclusion that we want to have, and how it

shouldn't be another generation of photo opportunities and plati-
tudes that replace real action.

With that in mind, I want to transition into a discussion of what
our priorities are at ITK and how they relate to self-determination.
We adopted our strategy and action plan earlier this year [2016]; it's
between 2016 and 2019, so it guides our organization for the next
three years. We have seven objectives within our strategy and action
plan, and the first one is in relation to suicide prevention. We released the National Inuit Suicide Prevention Strategy in July, and in
it we want to change the way Inuit and the rest of Canada think about
our interaction with suicide and suicide prevention. Canada was
focused this spring on Attiwapiskat and other Indigenous suicide
stories; it was even an emergency debate in the House of Commons,
in which many parliamentarians talked about the need for action. A
lot of the discussion was based on a couple of different things: first,
an individual perspective on what is a public health policy issue. For
some reason, in this field, an individual perspective can replace
best-practice, evidence-based public policy. The second thing that I
noticed was that the answers seemed to lie with those most affected,
and the issues were focused around the time when people are in crisis. The country wants to think about this issue as one that affects
Indigenous youth and they want to talk about this through the lens
of attempts and completions. I don't think that we deal with any of
our public health policies like that. The World Health Organization
says that suicide is a largely preventable public health crisis, and in
Quebec there is a strategy that has lowered the rate of youth suicide
by over half in the last twelve years—it is possible. We know that we
come from a low suicide reality: elevated rates of suicide only started
happening in the late 1970s. We were empowered by this data, this
evidence, so we set out to create an evidence-based, Inuit-specific

suicide prevention strategy that's globally informed, evidence-based, and Inuit-specific. And the outputs of it—and this is where it comes to self-determination—it's the idea that we won't get where we need to go without social equity. Housing, education, and health care are the key foundations of social equity; but when we have 40 per cent overcrowding rates for housing, when our educational attainment rates are approximately 30 per cent high school graduation for the adult population, and when we have 250 times the tuberculosis rates of all other Canadians born in Canada, we have a long way to go in achieving social equity.

We have huge challenges that then spur on negative consequences at the community level and at the family level. We know that we have historical trauma; we know that many of us haven't had the ability or opportunity to heal from all those things that happened to us in the 1950s and 60s, and that now have been cast upon the subsequent generations of Inuit. These things are not abstract: they are practical understandings of these concepts and of the inability for the Canadian public or government to accept that there's cause and effect. Even before we talk about mental health services or providing specific care to all those who are in need, and to do all that we can to safeguard people who are at risk—those are all necessary, but they are secondary in many ways to a transformational societal shift that needs to take place, to ensure we are not creating risk factors for suicide. If you live in Inuit Nunangat, you and your children are at a higher risk for suicide. And it doesn't matter how many protective factors you have, or how successful you are, or how strong your personal mental health is, the fact that we are encompassing entire populations with risk factors that then spill into society means that no matter who you are, you are affected: you know somebody who's died by suicide, or you have been put in situations where there has been crisis, or you or your family members have been abused. Fifty per cent of Inuit women in the 2008 Nunavut Inuit Health Survey reported being sexually abused in childhood; that is a reality, and it is unacceptable, and we need to change it.

All of these different things came together to create the National Inuit Suicide Prevention Strategy, and we did this together. It wasn't a couple of people at ITK that created this document: the Alianait Mental Wellness sub-committee, the Mental Health Commission of Canada, Health Canada, especially with support from their First Nations and Inuit Health Branch, and the board of ITK, and the National Inuit Committee on Health (of which there are members here today), all worked on this together, and it is our statement to Canada. And, once again, with this we are saying that this is what we want; and what's interesting in this time of reconciliation and self-determination is, how is Canada going to perceive that? How about the academics in this room whose field is mental health? Are you going to pick it apart? Are you going to say it's not really what Inuit want? Or perhaps a part of it is good, but the rest of it, you know, it could be improved? Or will you accept this is what Inuit have said to Canada, this is what we need, and work with us to achieve that goal through the way in which we have decided to move toward it? The way in which everyone—all Canadians—can play a role in Inuit self-determination is to accept that we have things to say, and that we do it in a way that respects our people and also respects human knowledge. The fact is that our suicide prevention strategy is globally informed and evidence-based. But that can sit right alongside "Inuit-specific," and there doesn't have to be a qualification there. It all matters; and why wouldn't we use the best of the world and the best of what we know, but also know our communities and ourselves well enough to know that things might not work even if they've worked in other places? So in suicide prevention, the way forward in self-determination is through listening to Inuit.

We talked about housing. Housing is our second priority, and I want to also think about self-determination in housing. For most of Canada the idea of housing is that there's a private housing market, then there's also a rental market, then there's social housing; and people usually float between those three in their lifetime. Perhaps in university you're in a dorm, so you're in an assisted rental situation. Those markets and that structure came to be over the course of the history of Canada, but housing in Inuit Nunangat, and the infrastructure in Inuit Nunangat writ large came about in fits and starts and wasn't ever meant to be a long-term solution. We're not a people that had private housing markets before contact, and before core settlement into our communities, so the idea that now we'd be able to figure it out in twenty or thirty or forty years is really a hindrance to the work that needs to be done. We still don't have a sustainable housing model.

In parts of Inuit Nunangat we have private home ownership, yet the majority of our people live in social housing. There is not a true sustainable transition into any other form of housing. The task in front of us today is to understand that there is a massive need—40 per cent overcrowding, as I've mentioned. There's also a question on the best housing design that hasn't been answered, and you can get into as much discussion as you want about the cool new innovative designs for housing, but that still doesn't get us to a sustainable housing solution. It is a component of it, but the idea for southern Canada is that you build equity through your home—it is an essential building block for your own personal worth—and then it is something that you pass on to future generations and it accumulates wealth over time. That is the model. For Inuit, what is the model? How do we create a sustainable housing structure? Next week there'll be an Inuit housing summit and we'll talk about these issues, but these are also academic questions as well. Perhaps there are solutions that we haven't thought of yet; perhaps there are partnerships to be had. But the idea of self-determination and housing is not that we just need a lot of money, and that we need to keep building the same sort of structures and the same governance models that we already have. It is to re-imagine what is possible and try and go ahead and achieve it. It's the same thing for infrastructure. Think about who built the infrastructure in Inuit Nunangat. A lot of it was built by the US military, who proved in the late [19]40s and early 50s that you can build long-term sustainable infrastructure in the Arctic. We still don't have that second wave that fills in from that first wave, which was dominated by Cold War considerations and by a government that isn't our own. All those Distant Early Warning sites that we pass when we're going on our trips on the land, or the airstrips that we probably fly onto every time we go to Goose Bay or to Iqaluit, who do you think built those, and what does it say about our place within Canada that we don't have a second phase of infrastructure being built in Canada that is intended to sustain our communities and society?

The third objective within ITK's Strategy and Action Plan is reconciliation, and this is an interesting one. The Government of Canada has made it their priority to talk about reconciliation and has done very unilateral things in this process. You think of on day one the name change from Aboriginal and Northern Affairs, I think it was, or Northern Development, to Indigenous and Northern Affairs, yet we didn't work with the government to change that name. There is no letter that you can find from the three Indigenous groups in Canada that says we request that the Government of Canada start using the term "Indigenous" instead of "Aboriginal." Just think about that point: it shows the transparency of where we are today, rather than the communicated space that the federal government wants to have with us that is one of empathy and sympathy and working together and partnership and renewed relationship. I believe that's possible. I believe we'll get there. But reconciliation isn't easy, and it isn't changing terms to fit your political goal.

Reconciliation is not just something that you do today that you didn't do yesterday: it is premised on action. The Missing and Murdered Indigenous Women and Girls inquiry, or the Truth and Reconciliation Commission's ninety-four calls to action, or the United Nations Declaration of the Rights of Indigenous Peoples: their acceptance and implementation are two different things. Accepting that they exist and saying that they're important allows for the Government of Canada and Canadians to think that we're actually doing something, when it isn't until we have implementation plans, and we have actions associated with each one of these things that are done from the ground up with Indigenous peoples, including Inuit Tapiriit Kanatami and our land claim organizations, that we actually are doing something different than we did yesterday. And that's where reconciliation breaks down. Everyone wants in on reconciliation today, but they often want in on non-Indigenous terms. You don't want true partnerships; you just want to be branded with that term and feel good about the fact that you're doing something for us, or with us. My central tenet on reconciliation is: it's not as easy as it looks, and it should be hard. Think about the residential school existence and the entirety of the residential school structure, then juxtapose that with other cultural genocide events that happened across the world. And we think about the lack of change in the way that we talk about our history and the individuals that are within our history, based on what we know now about the true intent of residential schools, and the fact that there were whistleblowers in the 1920s—there were people who spoke out against the treatment of Indigenous peoples. But there wasn't action; and there were actually people who were in charge of implementing these racist policies that killed thousands of children, and yet our history books don't change to reflect the enormity of that atrocity; that no individuals have to bear the guilt for that history, that somehow within Indigenous peoples still remains a societal issue. I would hope that if I did anything like what happened, that if I was responsible for anything like what happened to those children in those residential schools, that history would not treat me kindly, and that the good deeds that I've done would today be recast into the reality of the actions that I let happen. And I hope that we all would think that of ourselves—that the things that we do today, some of them may seem to be wrong in the future: like "oh, I really shouldn't have supported that particular program" or "those socks look awful on me." You have these things where you regret things in the future, but then there are objective truths; and the truth we find out over time, that many researchers in this room have helped uncover. And that's when we have to think differently about our past and about the people whom we lift up, and the people that we still consider to be heroes, and the new place that we have to then reconcile with. So I hope that reconciliation does include a change in the way people think about those past actors, because the world has accepted nothing less in other places where genocide has happened, and it should be the same here in Canada.

Point number four is in relation to education. It's interesting that reconciliation and education in our Strategy and Action Plan come together, and I've already talked a little bit about not accepting the present when it comes to education. I've given this example before, and just think about this: I have a nine-year-old and a seven-year-old;

Panigusiq is nine and Jushua is seven. They were lucky enough to be able to go to daycare in Inuktitut; that isn't a reality that all Inuit children can have. They can go to school in Inuktitut from Kindergarten to Grade 4, but there is nowhere in Canada where I can move and my child can then continue to go to school in his first language beyond Grade 4. The first day of school last year, when my eldest was going to Grade 3, and this was before I became ITK president, he had asked me: "Can we move somewhere where I can still go to school in Inuktitut?" And to think that I would have to go to Greenland to make that happen makes no sense.

Sixty per cent of all Inuit in Canada, no matter how much language loss we have, still say that Inuktitut is our mother tongue. The fact that we cannot create a bilingual education system is our failing, and it's our failing of our children; it isn't the failing of the federal government or a province or a territory by itself. It is what our parents and our grandparents wanted for us, and it's something that we have to do more to achieve. So the issues are: why do we have education? What is K through 12 education for? What do our communities want for our children—what skills and abilities do we want them to have by the time they're eighteen? And if you empower local communities to answer those questions and to create curriculums that satisfy those questions with answers that empower our society and our communities, then we'll have real success, not only in our K–12 system but also our early childhood development and on to post-secondary.

The world's leading institutions in post-secondary—the students who go to them don't come from one reality. There are a myriad of ways to get the skills necessary to compete in a global environment and to get the best quality education. Often we have not thought beyond the things the service delivery agents can provide. Teacher accreditation: Is there any magic in a four-year B.Ed.? Not to put down anyone who's taken it and who's become a wonderful teacher from it. But it was only the 1970s that many people who were taught in Canada were taught by teachers who went to normal school for a year, and then were taught on the job in a sort of apprentice-style manner, who have become amazing teachers and have successfully taught the children who went through those systems and then on to post-secondary and lead Canadian society today. But somehow we are stuck in saying that we don't have enough teachers, we don't have enough teachers who speak Inuktitut, and we don't know how to get from here to there without massive influxes of cash, to teach the same way that we are already teaching when there are other ways to do it. I'm going off script I think from the positions ITK has at the moment, but I'm doing that with a purpose; I'm putting this to the room, so [that] some of these things will be discussed in a new way. This is an academic setting: we are in a university. What do you do in post-secondary learning? What do you do within all of higher education? You contemplate questions and you try to find answers that move our societies forward. So this is what I'm trying to do today.

Priority five of seven in our Strategy and Action Plan is the environment. Last week I was on CBC's *Power and Politics*, and I hopefully was heard by more than just my social media following, and in it I talked about reconciliation and climate change being just as close a fit as the economy and climate change. Minister [Catherine] McKenna, the prime minister [Justin Trudeau], many different jurisdictions have talked about the need to link climate change and the economy. Now, whatever you think of that concept you should also be thinking of the concept of reconciliation and climate change, because isn't this one of the foundational tenets of our differences between non-Indigenous Canadians and Indigenous Canadians: the way that we treat the environment, the way that we look at our natural world, the love that we have for the species that live within our environment, the fact that we consider ourselves a part of our environment and that we do not dominate or control it? The idea that they would also be concerned about our health and our well-being, and our wish to ensure that our environment stays intact—those are new concepts. And so I would say that that would be a reconciliation moment, if the Government of Canada and provinces and territories, and all Canadians, would just accept that the way in which we interact with our environment, and the way in which climate change will affect us, is foundationally and fundamentally different in the way it will affect them. It isn't about gas going up another ten cents; it isn't about not being able to skate on the Rideau Canal for two more weeks during the year. This is about the entirety of our society staying intact, and I don't think that today there is a great enough appreciation for that.

Priority six is in relation to research, and this is something that we talked about this morning. We had a panel on self-determination in research, so we had panelists from across Inuit Nunangat talking about what activities we're undertaking in relation to self-determination and research. But at the national level, and at our level, we still don't have the ability to partner and participate in research the way that we need to. There are no Inuit on governing councils and Tri-council and any one of the agencies. Now, we can be excluded from the room because of a credentials argument, even though we do have credentialed people. There are Inuit in all sorts of fields, so I will never say there is no Inuk that hasn't earned a master's or doctoral degree, because there are. But the idea that we don't have a right to be in the room when the Tri-council agencies—an agency of government that has political control from ministers responsible for allocating funds, and then providing high-level strategic direction—just says that it's okay for them to bend their own rules that suit their governance model, but when it comes to us it's a hard and fast reality; that no, no we couldn't do that, we couldn't provide Inuit representation at the highest levels of the Canadian Institutes of Health Research or the Social Sciences and Humanities Research Council because that isn't how it works. But somehow a minister is able to completely change the direction of the way in which these organizations run and function.

This is the challenge that we face: it's a combination of knowledge and shared purpose, but also respect. So there is a shared purpose: we want the best for our research; we have a multitude of research questions that we need answered. We don't even know the ideation rates for suicidality in our regions. In the creation of our Inuit suicide prevention strategy, we had to go and dig through coroner data to even get the rates of Inuit-specific suicide in each one of our regions; we had to do that ourselves. We have basic gaps in knowledge. We also have a basic lack of respect for our people in the governance models that then dictate how monies are spent, and who gets them. These are things that need to change. Part of this dream that we all, I think, have to have about self-determination is that the constructs about who's in and who's out have to change. The idea that we are excluded from rooms because we aren't the foremost expert that is peer-reviewed, that has been selected by a panel to take one space within fifteen, versus we have knowledge that, no matter how smart you are in a non-Indigenous setting, you will never know the Inuit reality in the way that Inuit know it. That is the fundamental shift that I hope we can all see, and that is the self-determination approach to research that I hope we can usher in, in this new era of Inuit to Crown and nation to nation.

The last point on self-determination is in relation to health and well-being. Inuit get tired of hearing about the gaps in outcomes, and that our rates—actually, our rates drive researchers to us. There are very few places in the world where you can have research findings that attract a national interest because they're so bad, and there are such broad discrepancies between the Inuit-specific reality and the Canadian reality. And so, yes, these are questions that need to be answered, but it goes beyond that. We have a better understanding now of our health condition. We understand what we need to do to try to solve it. The question is: How can we work in partnership with governments to create the solutions that we know are necessary?

I think that we'll look back on this time as hopefully the end of inaction. I'm a huge fan of Cindy Blackstock and the work that she does for the First Nations Caring Society and for all Indigenous children. If you think about the specific things that organization has uncovered about the basic inequity between what is spent on Indigenous children versus spent on non-Indigenous children in one particular point in our health and social services spectrum, I think that you would imagine if we had 100 Cindy Blackstocks there would be 100 different examples that are equally powerful. That is the challenge of our time as well, to create social equity within health and our social reality that allows for us to move forward, and take advantage of self-determination in a way that our ancestors did, in a way that we know that we can moving forward.

I appreciate your attention here today. I hope that we can work together moving forward, and I also thank all of you in this room who have done amazing work on behalf of, with, and for Inuit. Nakummek.

Inuit Youth Today*

Maatalii Aneraq Okalik

Nakurmiik, Honourable Minister [Sean Lyall, then Minister of Culture, Tourism and Recreation in Nunatsiavut], and Tom [Gordon] as well. I'm so pleased to be here at the twentieth Inuit Studies Conference, and I have to say I've been to former conferences in the past, and I've had many colleagues who've played a meaningful role as presenters at former conferences; however, this is the best one to date, and the reason I say that is because it is very clear that when Inuit are equal partners in any process, the outcome is amazing. This is the first conference where I've seen as many Inuit presenters, delegates, cultural performances, and I'm blown away with the fact that I feel like I'm in Inuit Nunangat. Walking around St. John's the last few days with so many Inuit, I guess I've heard some people say taking over the city, and I'm very proud of the Inuit from Nunatsiavut who we're closest to regionally, in seeing the Inuit youth performing with the Nain Brass Band as well as other very beautiful showcases, and I can't say how proud I am to be Inuk more than I am today here with you all. So I have the great honour and opportunity to share with you

---

*   Editor's Note: This chapter is based on a transcript and video of Maatalii Okalik's talk as it was delivered at the Inuit Studies Conference. It has been edited for readability, but otherwise it has been left largely in the format of an oral presentation.

my perspectives, as well as the realities and priorities of Inuit youth in Canada today.

As you're all aware there are approximately 60,000 Inuit who live in Canada, and have lived in Canada for more than 149 years—for thousands of years—and we have four incredible regions all of which I can now say I've been in, and celebrated being Inuk in, most recently having gone to Nunatsiavut and actually been to Hebron, a really incredible place. There are 160,000 Inuit around the world and 60,000 here in Canada, with the majority of the Inuit population being Inuit youth. Where you see our communities on the map isn't necessarily where we have chosen to live and call home for the last at least sixty to seventy years. But as I indicate on many fronts, we call home not only the land we live on but the water and the ice which we've traversed and thrived off for thousands of years. We're strategically placed but we're incredibly adaptable, and we continue to be here today as Inuit, and that in itself I believe is something to celebrate. And as I often say, "We are Inuit, and we are still here." So as the honourable minister indicated, in this role I have the honour to serve with the Inuit Tapiriit Kanatami [ITK] board of directors, the four land claim regional presidents, the National Inuit Women's representatives, as well as our national Inuit president, Natan Obed—who has switched seats and is now sitting over here. I'd like to recognize our national president for his incredible work within the last year of his term.

But I also have the great honour to work alongside amazing Inuit from all of our regions who serve the National Inuit Youth Council. The National Inuit Youth Council was created in 1993 and has representation from each regional Inuit association across Canada with individuals who serve as youth coordinators in those respective organizations, and those six youth coordinators make up the majority of the council and elect a president every two years. So I've been in my role for about a year and a half and my term is up next June, so the Inuit youth in the room: start putting together your applications because this position will be opening next summer.

I wasn't really going to do this initially, but I think it's important for us to reflect on the past as we decide today what it is that we'd like to do as self-determined individuals which will of course mark our futures. As I was putting my presentation together, watching this five-minute video, I was reminded of why things are the way that they are today, the good and the bad, which I'll be able to unpack for you a little bit more following this video. As many are aware John Amagoalik was one of the negotiators for the land claims agreement that we have in Nunavut and this is an interesting snippet from the [19]70s game show that used to be shown on the national network, and he's trying to explain then what it is that Inuit were doing at that time and why, and I think it's incredibly important that we remember that, and honour that, and so if you have the patience I'll be playing this five-minute clip.*

That was the burden that Inuit youth at that time in the [19]70s had to face, and ultimately you heard with your own ears just now that what Inuit wanted at that time was to reclaim their self-determination as a people, to ensure that we had the opportunity and place within this colonial society—not post-colonial but colonial society—to be able to govern ourselves, as well as make decisions about our daily lives the Inuk way. It's very clear with that exchange that there's a western way of knowing and an Inuit way of knowing. And this is a clip from 1976, but I have to admit in my relations and my advocacy

---

*   Editor's note: At this point Ms. Okalik shows a short, recorded segment from the CBC show *Front Page Challenge*, originally broadcast in 1976, featuring John Amagoalik, negotiator for the Nunavut land claim. See http://www.cbc.ca/archives/entry/deciphering-inuit-land-claims.

I have the very same conversations today in 2016. "What is it that you want?" the host asked; and he answered very elegantly, "whatever is left of what we had before." We still want that today: we'd like to protect as much as possible of what we have left. When asked if they think it's a possible task—as I said earlier in my opening, we are Inuit and we are still here. We've come a long way, based on the legacy of the Inuit youth who had to champion our rights and interests in the [19]70s and up to today; and I have to say on behalf of Inuit youth, thank you for that. He also said that it's very difficult to quantify what it is that we want, but he put the power at the community level. We know that our strength lies with our communities, and we know that a lot of the solutions to the issues that we are trying to combat together lie in our communities, and we have a lot of front-line community leaders here in this room today, so I acknowledge you. But ultimately it was indicated in that short clip that the original intent for our mobilization, despite the trying times that we were facing—and this isn't long ago: I walk by John Amagoalik every single day on my way to work in Iqaluit, this is not old history—but today we are still interested in and dedicated to the survival of our people, and I have the opportunity to now share the Inuit youth priorities that came from the community level to the national level at the tenth National Inuit Youth Summit that we hosted in Iqaluit last August.

Inuit youth are interested in continuing to strengthen the relationship with our language. As an Indigenous population in Canada—and I say this every time—we pride ourselves for having the highest retention of our Inuit language, our original language, compared to other Indigenous peoples in this country. However, we do recognize it is on the decline. There is a lot of strength from region to region, but there definitely needs to be a concerted effort to ensure that our language survives and thrives. And I definitely see a day where Inuit, all Inuit, speak Inuktitut again, that Inuit parents are raising their children in Inuktitut, that we're working in Inuktitut, and that other individuals living in our homeland are learning and speaking Inuktitut with us.

The second priority is Inuit culture and practices. Yes, I am wearing a Marciano dress, and I'm standing in this lecture hall with you, but I enjoy hunting, and working with our skins, and learning from leaders who have continued those practices; like just looking at Elisapi Aningmiuq from Iqaluit—she opens her home to anybody who'd like to learn how to clean skin; Jeannie Kullualik advocating for Inuit language at the national level. There's so many leaders in this room who do this every day because it's important, because we know that it's something we'd love to continue to practice. And Inuit youth are interested in learning, Inuit youth want to learn, but we have to create that space for Inuit youth to have access to it, so that they themselves, we ourselves—the fastest growing population, the young population can raise and pass these traditions and practices to the next generation to come. It's up to us to provide that space for them, and I hope we can honour that.

Suicide prevention. We have the highest rate of suicide in the country, and in the world. Inuit youth recognize that and have a vested interest in reversing that statistic.

Education and empowerment: both in western epistemology and success that we recognize today in Canada through high school and post-secondary education, but as well through our Inuit ways of knowing, rooted in our language, culture, and practices.

And, of course, reconciliation. I spoke a bit about language before, but I'm getting personal now, and I'm showing some personal accounts. Just this past February I harvested my first caribou. As many of you are aware, in the region I'm from we have a moratorium, so we don't have the ability to harvest caribou there. Although I'm studying Political Science, I put this education to much higher esteem. I learned so much, and I was taught by a twenty-three-year-old Inuk youth. I learned a lot of Inuit words and terminologies that I wouldn't have unless I was going through this experience. He was really concerned because I said, "I will butcher this caribou; you will teach me by doing the one over there, but I will do this one," and he was like, "Are you sure?" And I said, "Yes, I would love to learn; I need to do this so that I can continue." And so I did, with his guidance. And I also learnt Inuit practices such as washing my hands in the stomach lining so the acid would kill the bacteria on my hands. And you know I could talk about that, but if it's not a peer-reviewed article, it's not deemed relevant or legitimate in the research world. But I encourage researchers in the room, and I know many of you do this in practice, but we have to find a way to ensure that our research and our ways of knowing are not only just as legitimate but more legitimate, because we're still here by virtue of that knowledge. And so, ultimately, I bring this up, also apart from research, Inuit youth are craving this. And you know our way of being has changed: we all have to work to pay bills, and so on. But for decision makers in the room and leaders in the room and for those tuning in, let us do our best to create that space for Inuit youth to continue these practices. It's suicide prevention, it's combatting mental illness, it's promoting mental wellness.

I can confidently state that Inuit youth today are in an interesting time whereby many suffer from an identity crisis, and that is because of the history that we have, that's not eons ago or hundreds and hundreds of years ago; this is a history, a living history, that is very close to us today. At the National Inuit Youth Summit a representative working at the Qikiqtani Inuit Association did an "Inuit History

101"—it was kind of a plenary session like this, and all the Inuit youth that were delegates of the summit sat in and learnt of that brief history. And I can say it was an aha moment for the Inuit youth in the room: "Oh that's why things are the way they are today," "Oh that's why I can't speak Inuktitut," "Oh that's why education wasn't necessarily a priority in my household, because of the relationship or experience my parents had in residential school." Someone said, "Oh that's why my mom couldn't ever tell me she loved me, because the right to parent was stripped from that generation just before ours." But with that knowledge and education and experience, Inuit youth, I think, everyone pledged in the room at that time, "I'm going to be that first generation who reverses those negative experiences and negative cycles, and create positive ones for my future generation that will follow me." Part of that reconciliation is having the space to be able to practice our Inuit culture and celebrate our Inuit culture, because Inuit youth today are very proud to be Inuk, we're a part of that process.

Suicide prevention. Again in history this is also something relatively new. I've taken an excerpt from the National Inuit Suicide Prevention Strategy [NISPS] that was released on July 27 of this year [2016] which indicates that the rate of suicide ranges from five to twenty-five times the rates of other Canadians in Canada, and that is even more profound on the international level, where we're at the forefront of the statistics. Inuit youth want to see suicide eradicated, but we know that there are solutions to this epidemic. One of those solutions, and I'm quoting NISPS here, is the removal and eradication of the social and economic inequities that we face here in Inuit Nunangat. Thirty-nine per cent of Inuit homes in Inuit Nunangat are overcrowded, versus 4 per cent of homes in the rest of Canada. That is substantial, and that has an impact on Inuit youth lives on a daily basis, where we have fourteen people living in a two- to three-bedroom home. Just imagine sleeping and waking up and getting ready for the day. I was in Europe last week and my room was really, really small, and it was very difficult—I know, first-world problems—but it was very difficult for me to just do regular things. I know that's a ridiculous example to try and pair with what I'm saying now, but this is a reality. Seventy per cent of homes in Nunavut don't have enough food to eat, versus 8.3 per cent of homes in the rest of Canada; that is substantial. If people don't have enough food to eat, how are they going to school and doing well in school and succeeding? How are parents able to put a priority on healthy lifestyles and promoting Inuit language and culture, when they're surviving, just getting by, figuring out how to pay bills and buy food? These are just some of the social and economic inequities that we face. I mentioned that I was in Europe last week, and it was for a United Nations meeting around the Sustainable Development Goals [SDGs], which are global goals that all member states with the United Nations have pledged or hoped to achieve. But they're not new: they came from the Millennium Development Goals [MDGs] created in 2000, to achieve zero poverty, food security, and healthy homes and communities by 2015. But the Millennium Development Goals were created for developing countries, and when I was at Carleton and learning about the MDGs, I was like, "But this is what's happening in Inuit Nunangat—this doesn't make sense." And I actually had a lecture with my professor (he carried the charter of the UN in his breast pocket) where we debated, and I was just like, "This can be applied to Canada; while Canada is a developed country, this still can be applied to Canada; this is happening where I'm from." Well, Canada's a veto nation, has veto power at the United Nations, so no, this is not the way that it is. So when the UN *rapporteur* on special issues would come to Canada thereafter, and would put a line in there about Inuit suffering from food insecurity or overcrowded homes, I started sending those links to my professor saying, "See, this is what I'm talking about." But there is a lack of awareness about that. When there is a decision being made not by Inuit, or in concert with Inuit, in Ottawa, when this information is not made available or people don't know this, and when only 1 per cent of Canadians have been to Inuit Nunangat but are making decisions on our future, that's problematic.

I believe that once this is a national position, once these social and economic inequities are addressed, once they're eliminated and Inuit live the same way that other Canadians live but in our way of living, then I think that suicide numbers would decrease substantially, if not be eliminated. A few weeks ago, I and a number of other Inuit youth testified to the House of Commons Standing Committee on Indigenous and Northern Affairs specifically about suicide. At that time there was Nina Ford from Nunatsiavut who testified, Alicia Aragutak, and Louisa Yeates from Nunavik and myself, and we had to bring to the forefront some of the things I've just identified, and it was a shocker for the Standing Committee members who were there, the House of Commons MPs. I said at that time, "the very people who occupied your seats not so long ago would be happy about this— this would be good news; because the policies that they created and implemented at the national level on us, the very purpose of those policies was for us to become non-Inuk in a way, for us to no longer be able to speak our language, for us no longer to live the savage life that I hold near and dear to my heart today, and, although unwritten, maybe for us no longer to exist." And that's a fact. But I said, "We're here, though, and you have to work with us to be able to address the issues that we face on a daily basis because we're an asset: we assert sovereignty to northern Canada, we occupy and live off the coastline that you call your home; but geopolitically it just doesn't make sense—

our state of affairs is just not appropriate." But I ultimately stated that suicide is 100 per cent preventable, and that it's a national issue that requires a national response.

Another priority, the fourth that the National Inuit Youth Council has, is education and empowerment. And as I said, we have to look at education not only as western epistemology but also the Inuit ways of knowing, but also reflective of our time. And so one thing that we like to do through the National [Inuit] Youth Council is to create awareness and empower each other, and I'm so pleased that my former keynote speakers have indicated an interest, and a celebration really—when we as Inuit work together, we as Inuit celebrate together, and empower one another—we can't afford not to at this point. And so we publish the national Inuit youth magazine called *Nipiit*, and regions have the opportunity to share what it is great that's being done in our communities, and across all fifty-three communities. Despite the negative statistics, there are a lot of amazing things happening. As well—I didn't think I was going to do this but because we just did talk about suicide—we released with ITK and Economic Club of Canada the Inuit-youth-specific financial literacy toolkit, because we do recognize that it is 2016, and there's a way of doing business today: we have bills that we need to pay, and some financial stressors actually are [the] cause of a lot of the issues that Inuit youth are facing, whether it be mental health issues, stress, or anxiety. But this is not only an Inuit youth reality in Canada—financial issues, I think we all have once faced, or continue to face. And so what we want do is empower Inuit youth through education and tools, so we created this Inuit-youth-specific financial literacy toolkit. And it's as simple as how to get a SIN number or how to open a bank account. Those are all simple things, but we don't have banks and institutions in all of our fifty-three communities; some people are merely holding cash and using cash. And how to save money is something that's included in there, as well as how to build on your own earning potential. And the reason why we're keen on this piece was because—what I'm wearing right now, this piece created by my sister-in-law, or this sealskin cuff—the way that we see returns based on our economies is reflective of our culture, and so when a man hunts and harvests seal and feeds his family and community, to when Jeannie Kullualik, or like I said Elisapi Aningmiuq, clean the skin and teach me as an Inuk youth how to do that, and we soften and chew the skin to make our kamiik, and I was doing that alongside some of the women in this room, to when Inuit youth, both of whom made these two pieces, depend on that money to pay their bills today: that's why we were excited about having the financial literacy toolkit be reflective of who we are as part of honouring that education and empowerment priority. When the National Inuit Suicide Prevention Strategy was released, it was supposed to happen in Hebron, Nunatsiavut, but we know that *Sila* rules all and we're at her mercy. So when not everybody from the ITK board of directors and the federal government could come, we did have an event with the Students on Ice participants, and I saw some of the youth that were there, here in this room over the last few days. But as I said at our summit, Inuit youth—and not only Inuit youth, but Canadians—aren't aware of our history, and Hebron is a community that Inuit use to thrive in and call home, and I got to see some incredible sod house remnants, and there are some cabins that are there—the Moravian church, where Inuit were not allowed to throat sing and drum dance: we did that day, really excitedly, in the church. Inuit youth rebel, and activities like this foster that engagement and that dialogue; and yesterday Tanya Tagaq, and two days ago Natan said that the dialogue has to change. They're absolutely right, and this is an example of it. It's tough, it's very tough, it's very emotional: I was crying yesterday when Tanya spoke, I cried this morning when I watched that John Amagoalik clip—I don't usually cry that much, just so you know—but a lot of Inuit and Canadians, and there were international students on this expedition, were like, "Oh my God, I had no idea." And that's usually the response I get when I'm addressing groups like yours. Both Inuit and non-Inuit just need to have that dialogue. Because not until Inuit youth know can they critically analyze their surroundings and decide how they'd like to contribute to their communities in a way that is positive, and a way that is reflective of what we hold near and dear and at the core of our being as Inuit, and that's our culture. And so this was a celebration of that.

So the last priority that we have is reconciliation. This was identified in all of the keynotes over the last few days, and it's something that I think is all-encompassing and requires a holistic approach. We're aware of the great work that's been done with the Truth and Reconciliation Commission [TRC], and that was a call nationally for Indigenous peoples in Canada to have the opportunity to talk about that experience. Because my mom went to residential school, that generation went to residential school, and although there wasn't necessarily an Inuit leadership presence in that process, Inuit still had the opportunity to talk about it, and can see ourselves reflected in the ninety-four calls to action that came out of that experience. I've been pointing to one particular call to action from the Inuit youth perspective, which is TRC number 66: "We call upon the federal government to establish multi-year funding for community-based youth organizations to deliver programs on reconciliation and establish a national network to share information and best practices." Many of you have found in your research and recognized, that the solution lies with our communities and the community strength that we have across all fifty-three. I see strength in this particular call to action because I saw success in the Aboriginal Healing Foundation work that was being done at the community level, and I truly believe that if this particular call to action is honoured, that Inuit youth will be better set in being able to do what they like to do in their communities around reconciliation, and that, as I stated, could lie in the other priority areas that Inuit youth have identified nationally.

But I also see reconciliation coming outside of just that particular directive, and it is reflected in some recent news headlines. The *Ottawa Citizen* reported on my recent testimony to the Senate Standing Committee on Aboriginal People. I said to them a lot of what I've been saying now. I also spoke about the Prime Minister's Youth Council, and I have been asking prior to the PM's election and throughout his term so far—I guess it's one year coming up—how Inuit youth were going to be reflected in federal business. And it was indicated before that the Prime Minister's Youth Council would be created. I had met with the secretariat, as he serves as the minister responsible for youth, and I indicated a lot of the barriers for Inuit youth across Inuit Nunangat to even be considered to serve on that council. How effective that council will be we do not know at this time, but if Inuit youth aren't reflected in the membership of that council then all of the statistics that I've identified as being problematic, that affect us on a daily basis, cannot be properly addressed when federal policy is being discussed with this body. So, why is it that we always have to fight for a seat at the table?

Another recent news item featured Natan Obed, commenting on Canada's climate strategy and implementing the Paris Agreement, and Inuit not being at the table for that, despite us being the human face of climate change. Yet another recent headline declared: "The new Inuit-Crown relationship remains undefined, leaders say," and that came out of the ITK annual general meetings we had in Kuujjuaq just a few weeks back. I really think reconciliation means that these headlines are no longer read on a daily basis and that actual action is attached to solutions that we as Inuit identify in our communities.

Other headlines are about reconciliation. The three I just identified had to do with federal government issues, but this one touches ordinary Canadians: why are people dying because they're assumed to be drunk, when really they're having a stroke? That's embedded in that history over the last sixty to seventy years, and there's a lot of work that needs to be done, by all Canadians, on reconciliation and changing attitudes. Opening hearts and minds to our knowledge and who we are is one step, so that we don't read stuff like that anymore. Why is one of our most celebrated artists—why—you know I shouldn't even have to ask that question and that headline should not exist. So when Canadians ask me, "How can I help, how can I be a part of the reconciliation process?," I say first I recognize you're asking the question and that is the first step, and when you're doing your business on a day-to-day basis at the front lines no matter what it is that you're doing, keep us in mind and keep us as an equal partner and I think that things like this will no longer exist. When the prime minister says "because its 2015," about having an equal gender reflective cabinet, I want *that* expectation applied to *our* daily life. I want that to be celebrated when we do live the same way that our fellow Canadians live here in this country. That's an example of reconciliation. And this, within our communities, is reconciliation. The more we build each other up the stronger that we will be. We shouldn't have to gather only in times of crisis: we should also be gathering in times as we celebrate each other. I see it reflected in beautiful Inuit art like that of Annie Pootoogook [1969–2016, Canadian Inuk artist from Cape Dorset] and her relations, because that's who we are as Inuit.

And so I encourage Inuit to continue to come together and celebrate as we slowly work toward a brighter future.

I'm appreciative of the awards Inuit Tapiriit Kanatami have for our leaders in our fifty-three communities, and we were really happy to award Inuit youth Olivia Ikey for the incredible work that she's doing in her community in Kuujjuaq in Nunavik. We have to continue to foster Inuit language and ways of knowing within post-secondary streams, and we see the success in Nunavut Sivuniksavut [Ottawa college where Inuit students from the north study Inuit culture, history, and language] and we're really excited that Nunavik will have a model for themselves based in Montreal. The success of those institutions is because their curriculum has reflected what Inuit youth see themselves in, or strive to achieve, and that, as I said, is Inuit language and culture. I was at the One Young World Summit two weeks ago, and there was Senator Murray Sinclair talking about reconciliation at an international level. Not only do we require community strength within Inuit communities but we also need it with our fellow Indigenous peoples in Canada as we work toward this national objective. I really encourage reconciliation within our communities. And one thing I'm going to point to, because we have linguists and language specialists and language promoters in the room, for Inuit youth is: we do recognize the strength of many regions about language, but there are some Inuit youth in this room who cannot speak Inuktitut fluently. But it's not their fault, and we have to remember that, and we have to remind each other of that, and we have to continually encourage each other as we strive to be at 100 per cent proficiency level at Inuktitut in our communities. Unfortunately, what I've had to do, and it's very tough, is put myself out there, be very vulnerable, try to speak Inuktitut. And I have people who play a really incredible daily role for me when I see them about Inuit language, and to see how they raise their children in an Inuktitut-only-speaking home—that's life goals for me, and I can say that it's the life goals for Inuit youth today. But sometimes when I'm trying and I'm unsuccessful in my attempts, I have some people make fun of me—and, okay, I have thick skin, not only cause I'm Inuk, but because I had no choice living, growing up in Ottawa but to have thick skin. And what I have found as a positive reaction is, "How come you don't teach me instead of make fun of me?" Because if that happens, and I can imagine that happening every single day, someone can decide, "What's the point? Forget about it, I'm not even going to bother trying." And that is severing the lifeline of Inuktitut for many generations to come. But I'm very proud that I usually get these two responses: one, silence, because I called them out on that issue, or two, yes let's do this together. And some of the people who had a microscope on me in a negative way are my best teachers today. And so that is part of reconciliation in our communities as we continue to change that dialogue, and Inuit youth are a part of that change.

I have had the opportunity to outline the five priority areas of Inuit youth, and I encourage each one of you to take to heart what I've said. Because it doesn't just come from me: it comes from Inuit youth who participate at the summit and decide what it is that we need to discuss nationally and internationally. I encourage each one of you in your work—whether that's in research, community development, leadership, politics, and everything else in between—to remember that decisions made today will impact our future for hundreds and hundreds of years to come, and we have the opportunity to define what that future looks like. And just know that Inuit youth are with you and want [to] be a part of that process. So with that, *nakurmiik*, thank you, *merci*.

Inuit Women's Leadership:
A Nunatsiavut-Based Narrative

Andrea Procter, Beverly Hunter, and Charlotte Wolfrey

> *Women contribute a lot to the community and to the family.*
> *They're the leaders in the family, and they make the decisions.*
> *They're looked up to a lot [but] sometimes we feel like we're not*
> *being recognized.* (Rutie Lampe, interview, Nain, 2016)

Academic discussions about Inuit leadership in Nunatsiavut often re-
volve around formal governance structures, public authority figures,
and historical Inuit and Moravian traditions that prioritized male
leadership (Brantenberg 1977; Kleivan 1966; Procter 2016). But
when asked about Inuit women's leadership, Nunatsiavummiut offer
a different picture—one that re-defines notions of leadership itself.
Drawing on the collaborative project *Daughters of Mikak: Celebrating
Inuit Women's Leadership in Nunatsiavut*, this chapter presents a
chorus of Inuit voices that illustrate and honour the distinct leadership style of women in Nunatsiavut who create social networks that
withstand the impacts of colonialism.

The *Daughters of Mikak* initiative originated in 2014 as an idea
for a Nunatsiavut-university research project from community members such as Charlotte Wolfrey of Rigolet, who said that the region
has a long history of strong female leaders, but that they were often

underappreciated.[1] Andrea Procter, Charlotte Wolfrey, Beverly Hunter, and seven others formed an advisory working group for the project and discussed how to proceed.[2] We wanted to include as many people as possible in identifying female leaders in Nunatsiavut and to respect the Nunatsiavut sense of humility and preference not to boast about oneself (Briggs 1974; McGrath 1997). The group decided that the project should encourage Nunatsiavummiut to create tributes about Inuit women who have had a strong influence on their lives. Instead of asking people to talk about themselves, we helped them express their appreciation for others by making digital stories about inspirational Inuit women.[3] We left the definition of leadership open and aimed to merely provide a space for the discussion to occur.

The project was named *Daughters of Mikak* after a historical Inuit leader who has had an enduring legacy in the history of Labrador and who remains an example of a strong Inuit woman. In the late 1700s, Mikak was a central figure in the negotiations between Labrador Inuit, the British, and Moravian missionaries. Captured by the British and taken to London, where she met with various authorities, including royalty, she discussed the possibility of establishing a Moravian mission in Labrador with the missionary Jens Haven. After Mikak returned to Labrador, Moravian missionaries relied on her role as an ambassador and followed her advice to build the first mission station at Nain, in 1771 (Fay 2014; Stopp 2009; Taylor 1983, 1984). The female Inuit leaders featured in the *Daughters of Mikak* stories follow in Mikak's footsteps.

The project team encouraged Nunatsiavut community members to participate in the *Daughters of Mikak* project by recording audio tributes and adding photographs to create digital stories. These digital stories were then posted on the *Daughters of Mikak* Facebook page (www.facebook.com/DaughtersofMikak/), and the number of people who engaged in the project through "liking" the page and sharing the stories climbed steadily.[4] By July 2018, forty-four narratives had been created by people throughout Nunatsiavut and beyond. Most have been done by women (of the forty-four, four were made by men), and the majority (thirty-three out of forty-four) are about family members. Pieces run from one to six minutes in length, with an average time of about three minutes. Except for two stories that involve a video component, all are a combination of photographs and the narrator's voice-over. These digital stories have been viewed almost 42,000 times on Facebook, shared about 575 times, and reached more than 125,000 people. Given that fewer than 3,000 people live in Nunatsiavut, the *Daughters of Mikak* stories constitute a widely discussed narrative.[5]

NARRATIVE THEMES

The inspirational Inuit women chosen to be celebrated in the *Daughters of Mikak* project are diverse. Some are grandmothers, and some are young women. Some are politically active on a national level; some focus their efforts on their family members and neighbours. Some live in large urban centres, while some lived mainly with their family on the land. Despite the differences, common themes emerge.[6] The ability to create and maintain strong social connections between people, generosity, patience, humility, outspokenness, strengthening bonds through speaking Inuktitut and spending time together on the land, and a fierce perseverance are features deemed inspirational. In this chapter, we illustrate how the narratives outline the importance of creating relationships and strong social networks through each of these themes. We then discuss how the stories demonstrate a distinct style of leadership and how this leadership plays a role in shaping current Nunatsiavut society.

Relationships and mutual support

The stories illustrate how the *Daughters of Mikak* women create close ties with many people, but more specifically within families. Salome Jararuse explains how her mother, Selma Jararuse, works hard to unify their family:

> She's the rock of our family, she keeps us all together. She makes us stick together—she's very keen on that. Family is a very big thing to her. She likes to keep us all together and to lean on each other, to make sure we're always there for each other, to always love each other and to watch out for each other.

Many of the women create various family relationships with those around them. Alice Harris recounts how her grandmother, Emelia Merkuratsuk, played multiple family roles in her life: "She was my special person. I just loved her. My mother died when I was young. She was my mother and my grandmother." While some raised the idea that "family is first," importance is also given to expanding the boundaries of who is considered family. Some appreciated those who welcomed them or others into their family. For instance, Charlotte Wolfrey explains how Eva Palliser would take Charlotte on the land with her family when she was a child:

> In addition to raising her children, I had the privilege of tagging along on many of their going out on the land expeditions. I remember being able to go with them for sometimes weeks at a time.... This was a woman who had her own family, who had very little earthly possessions and absolutely no money (like everyone else at the time), yet she still made room for me in her boat, in her tent, in her life in every way.

Nakummek [thank you] Eva, Nulligivagit [I love you], or in Rigolet style, Nugligivagiit.

By making room for other people in their families, their homes, or their hearts, these women connect people by "lov[ing] them as her own," as Caroline Nochasak says of her grandmother, Sarah Nochasak:

> She's always willing to help, no matter what. My Anânsiak Sarah always had room in her home for family members and children, and loved them as her own, including me.... Being able to love everyone, no matter what, and being willing to help people just like that.

Miriam Brown, too, was celebrated for extending her family to include others who needed help, as her granddaughter, Rosina Brown, recounts:

> She was a foster parent, traditionally. Back in the day, there was a lot of people who, some of them had families who were too big, and so a lot of families couldn't take care of each other, so some of them would just go to live with other people in the community. There was a lot of people who would do this—it was a way of life. And so there was some people, and they'd go and live with Anânsiak.... I didn't know that they lived with her, because a lot of the time, this happened before my time, cause they're all older people, and they'd be on the road—"hey, Mom," "hi, Mom!" And to auntie, "hi, Sis!" [I would ask,] "Is that our family?" [She would answer,] "No." They went to live with Mom years ago.... She took a lot

of people in and a lot of times, it was because of hard times, like hardships, and families help each other out in times of need. So she was really good that way …

Helping those in need is a trait that is especially celebrated. The women are often admired for their willingness to help others, especially those who are facing a crisis.

She helped in our community by always being there to help others. If there was a tragedy, she always made sure she had time for those families who were suffering. I remember her always bringing leftovers to our neighbours, little small gestures she always did what she could to help other people…. She taught me that family is always first, to be kind to people, to take care of people that you love, and to help others who aren't so fortunate, and to just always make sure that your children know they are very loved by you. (Jessie Wyatt by Sandra Dicker)

Many stories involve a tribute to people who share with others and with those who are experiencing difficulties:

She was always kind, and she always shared whatever she wanted to with other people that were hungry or needed help. She would always share whatever she had with other people, and she cared about people. (Jenny Ikkusek by Nancy Ikkusek)

This help often involved thoughtfulness and kindness, in thinking of other people's needs, or looking after family members and children.

Marilyn Baikie portrays her mother, Sarah, as driven to extend help and a welcoming hand to everyone:

> She's the kind of person who just puts everyone ahead of herself. She would do anything to help anyone. It doesn't matter if it's part of her family, if it's part of her community, it doesn't matter if she even knows them, but she will go out of her way to make sure that everyone feels welcome and feels appreciated. If they need help, then she will make sure that someone is there to help them ... She just wants to help people and, not because it's of any reward to her, but she truly believes in her heart that that's what we're here to do, to help people, and the more we can help and the more good that we can do, the more good will come to us.

Forming and strengthening connections and relationships with people, in the ways that the *Daughters of Mikak* women do, create bonds of interdependence between people and feelings of responsibility for each other. Beyond the family and Nunatsiavut community level, forging relationships help people find their own Inuit grounding and identity, as Diane Obed expresses in her tribute to Zippie Nochasak. Diane, who lives in Halifax, tells how Zippie helped her to create relationships that helped her to ward off feelings of homesickness and instability:

> We developed a relationship when she was living here in Halifax ... Before she came here, I felt homesick a lot, just for home and family, and when she came, she provided the comfort of home and family, and just radiated love, joy, and community wherever she goes ... I saw that her heart is so

big that wherever she goes, she makes friends and people are just drawn to her light. She embodies the Inuk woman's motherly and grandmotherly spirit.... She's helped me to find lifelong connections and friendships that I will continue to benefit from ... in my life.

Modelling relationships: Generosity and patience

The stories illustrate not only how the women connect people but the ways in which they form social connections. Just as Zippie fostered "love, joy, and community," Beatrice Watts is described as creating strengthening and supportive ties:

> What I noticed about Mom was that she always had a kind word and the time to chat with people. She was the type of person who lifted people up. She didn't put people down, she didn't go around gossiping or saying mean things. She always saw the good in people. She always wanted to be there for people.... She was really always aware of other people.... She focused on the good in people, and brought out the best in people.... When I think of my mother, I remember the love. (Beatrice Watts by Gwen Watts)

Beatrice Watts formed these relationships by spending her time visiting with people:

> When I think about my mother, I think about the strong connections to people.... My mother always made time to visit, visit, visit, so I'd always spend lots of time with friends and relatives ... It was all in Inuktitut of course, and I'd be tagging along as her little ghost, and I'd be sitting down, just

soaking it all in, and it was just such a special, special time.…
Family was just everything to her.

Others detail similar ways in which the women modelled or
taught about creating supportive and healthy relationships. While at
least seven of the women were teachers in the formal schooling system, the majority taught those around them informally, often by
leading by example instead of explicitly instructing. In some of the
narratives, the women's patience was highlighted as a key aspect of
their teaching. Kristie Holwell's story about Maria Dicker illustrates
the importance of patience:

> Maria Dicker inspires me because she's a patient, fun, and
> natural teacher. Maria taught me how to clean my first seal-
> skin after I shot my first seal. She was more than happy, she
> was eager, and she was very patient in teaching me how to
> clean the fat off the sealskin, to drying and stretching the
> sealskin and sewing and making a pair of mitts.

Fran Williams recounts how her grandmother, Kitora Boase,
taught her about relationships with other people by modelling this
behaviour herself:

> My grandparents had a lot of influence on me. They taught
> me patience, to love the land, to be good to other people.
> They used to KaKak me all the time. She always used to make
> my tea in the morning although I was old enough to make it
> myself.… Her friends were Mrs. Nitsman and Eli. They often
> used to come to Anânsiak's in the evening to play cards.…
> After I went to bed, I would listen to them talking. I would

feel really secure, knowing that they were there in the kitchen. They used to treat me well—they used to treat me too well! [laughs]

Nancy Ikkusek explains how her mother, Jenny Ikkusek, showed her how to support other people; Nancy now follows her lead:

> She was important to me because she taught me right from wrong, and she always used to say, would you like to be treated like that? And she would say it in Inuktitut, and that would make *me* think that if I did something bad, I wouldn't want someone to do that to me.... She improved my life because I tried to do what she used to do—I try to share what I can with low-income families, and I try to listen or see who's hurting because that's what she would do.

For Megan Webb, it was her grandmother, Rose Webb, who modelled healthy and supportive relationships: "She taught me the happiness of life; she taught me don't take anything for granted. She was always someone that was there for me."

Humility and speaking truth to injustice

The patience and willingness to teach others that many identified in their narratives was mixed with a profound sense of humility and not wanting acknowledgement for personal accomplishments. Some narrators stressed that the women themselves would not have presented themselves with the same admiration: "Now in saying this, I do want to say that my mother would be the first to say that she's not perfect. She didn't like being praised up or made to be wonderful" (Beatrice Watts by Gwen Watts). Miriam Brown was equally self-effacing:

She was a humble woman, and when you look at it now, everything was kind of quiet, like whenever there was stuff that was happening that she should be recognized for, it just passed. She was happy to just let it pass, no matter how big an achievement or hard work she did.... She was a humble woman, don't like bragging about the stuff you did and do. (Miriam Brown by Rosina Brown)

Sharon Edmunds tells a similar story about her mother, Ruth Flowers:

She was absolutely an amazing woman. She wasn't looking for rewards. She wasn't looking for praise or admiration. She was just trying to make people's lives better. She didn't want any acknowledgement or fanfare—that wasn't her. She knew she made a difference.

Many of the women were not interested in individual praise or acclaim and do not want to brag or present themselves as any better than anyone else. This humility, however, does not translate into timidity. Several narratives identified women's courage in speaking their minds and in tackling injustice. Some described this outspokenness as being particularly impressive in a small number of older women, who would speak out in order to give moral advice when people were not behaving as they should.

[Sarah Nochasak is] also honest. She wasn't afraid to speak her opinion and give advice, so she's really blunt, and you can expect that from her. She would give advice and be angry out of love and just [give] constructive criticism. (Caroline Nochasak)

Julie Dicker recounts the same moral authority of her grand-mother, Sue Harris:

> Being true to herself and to everyone else around her is im-portant, too. Growing up, say we—or even now, say we do something wrong, or something she knows isn't right. She'd be the first one to tell us that, ok, don't do that, that just isn't right. You got to do it the right way.

Miriam Brown had similar ways of asserting her position, as Rosina Brown relates:

> She was very outgoing, very pleasant, very enthusiastic. She would just draw you to her—she was like a magnet, always happy. When she got mad, it was always in a good way, with a good point, but it was always with good intentions when-ever she got that way.

In similar fashion, Carlene Palliser portrays how her grandmother, Eva Palliser, had withstood attacks on her language and way of life and remained rooted in her culture. She drew strength from her cultural survival and could see things clearly and voice her insights:

> [Speaking Inuktitut, she] wasn't ashamed of their language. It was a large part of who she was and where she came from. Being there through all the changes in the culture and lan-guage, she never lost who she was. She always spoke the truth, even it if was something that someone didn't want to hear or agree with.

Silpa Edmunds was another woman who spoke her mind, especially when it came to inequity, as her grandson, Tyler Edmunds, explains:

> One of the strongest memories that I have of my grand-mother, she was very tenacious, she was very strong, she always spoke her mind—she was very blunt. If there were any injustices, anything she felt wasn't fair, she would be the first to speak out against it, and she would invest all of her time and energy into ensuring that she did what she could to try to rectify that, to try to fix it. Right until her dying day, she had that passion, that energy to try to speak out against injustices.

Beatrice Watts was equally outspoken, as Gwen Watts relates:

> She was an advocate on so many levels. She certainly fought all the time for anything to do with Inuit, and making sure that Inuit were treated fairly. And also that went for women, and Labradorians in general. She was a strong advocate, and I think of my mother as a kind, patient woman, but when she thought that people were being treated unfairly or that there was some injustice or prejudice, she became angry and she spoke up ... She wouldn't stand for anything that put down other people, particularly based on race, and she always stood up. So in general, kind and patient, but with injustices, she had a steel backbone, I tell you.

Relationships through Inuktitut and the land

Another common theme centred around speaking Inuktitut with each other and spending time together on the land. Charlotte Wolfrey chronicles her childhood learning experiences during the time she spent with Eva Palliser on the land:

> It was because of Eva I saw a Kullik being used in our tent. I saw bread being baked in the sand. While I was with her and her family, I spoke Inuktitut and I ate raw seal meat and seal fat. I was as free as a bird when I was with Eva and her family, I can't remember having to help with chores, I could play as long as I wanted, I learned to do things by watching.

Charlotte tells a story about speaking Inuktitut with Eva's family, and how they shared a laugh when she made up a name for mosquitoes that was half English, half Inuktitut—"nipper-ee." Sharing these experiences on the land, Charlotte and Eva's family built lifelong ties with each other in self-sufficient freedom from outside influences and control.

Speaking Inuktitut or working to maintain the language is considered a way of binding people together. Nancy Rose has fond memories of her childhood relationship with her foster mother, Nancy Pamak, in sharing Inuktitut and traditional sewing skills:

> The woman who inspired me the most was Nancy Pamak. She fostered me, she reared me up. And the best thing she used to do was be sewing sealskin, talking in Inuktitut to me. Sometimes I wouldn't understand when I was young, and she showed me how to understand it. I couldn't really speak it, but I could understand it. And that's the one woman that I love so much that inspired me the most.

Similarly, Tyler Edmunds cherishes the relationship that he developed with his grandmother, Silpa Edmunds, when he decided to learn Inuktitut:

> She was very passionate about the language, and she was a very strong advocate.... I was energized and I got a bit of passion from my grandmother for the need to pursue the language.... As I got older, I began to recognize the importance of the language. She reinforced that heavily for me. Anytime that she saw that I had some interest, she would throw herself behind it, one hundred per cent. Especially in the last few years that she was living, she was very proud of the efforts I was putting into it. Just that connection that we had, while we were learning it, it was definitely one of my best memories of her. Just that bonding that we created through the language itself. Any speakers of the language, when someone shows initiative in it, they want people to learn the language, they want to share their language, they want to have that connection.... You could see it in her eyes, when something was pronounced just right. She would become so proud. It's definitely one of my fonder memories, just that little connection that you would have in that moment, just sharing the language, and having that little bond.

Ellen Adams, an Inuktitut teacher in Rigolet, details how she developed a strong relationship with her grandmother, Elsa Palliser Adams, through spending time with her on the land and by learning Inuktitut from her:

I spent every summer with Gram and Gramps at our summer cabin at Sandy Cove, and also every chance I can during the winter at Carwalla. Gram is my inspiration because there is nothing she couldn't do. She could do everything that was expected of a woman—cook, clean, sew, make clothing, raise the children—but she also help[ed] with the wood, build the cabin, tend the nets, fish … the list goes on and on. Gram spoke Inuktitut both at home and in the community to her husband, friends, children, and grandchildren. My Gram was also Rigolet's very first Inuktitut teacher. She's the reason I'm here today following in her footsteps, passing on her knowledge. If I listen closely, I can still hear her calling on the CB: "Songmiatsimiut, songmiatsimiut, tusâvisi? [People of Back Run—do you hear me?]"

Both the vitality of Inuktitut and life on the land in Nunatsiavut have been heavily attacked over the last fifty years or so. The Inuktitut language was once much more widely spoken in Nunatsiavut, and Inuit used to spend more time on the land at fishing places, homesteads, and aullâsimavet, but compulsory schooling in English, forced relocations from northern Labrador, centralization into communities, increased state regulation of land- and sea-based life, and the collapse of the cod fishery have all contributed to this decline. The Moravian mission provided schooling in Inuktitut in Hebron, Nain, and Hopedale until the early 1950s, but the only option for many families south of Hopedale to obtain formal education was English-language residential or day schools. After Labrador joined Canada in 1949, the government instituted compulsory schooling in English. As Ellen Adams notes, Elsa Palliser Adams avoided losing her language because of family tragedy:

Elsa Palliser was born at English River on February 7, 1932. Her mother died at a very young age, and being the eldest daughter, the responsibility of raising the remainder of her siblings fell to her. As a result, she did not attend residential school. This, I think, was a major reason she was able to retain her Inuit culture, heritage, and language.

Many others attended English-language residential or day schools, and their use and understanding of the language often suffered. Gwen Watts relates how her mother, Beatrice Watts, resisted this process by using her Inuktitut to create relationships while she was in residential school:

> She had to go to school in North West River when she was 12, and she finished school there. So when she went down, you can imagine she was very homesick and lonely.... So what she did, we had the main hospital in North West River at the time, and that's where everyone came for their medical care, so as a child, she'd go over to the hospital looking for anyone from the north coast. She knew a lot of people, but then if she didn't, she'd just go up to them and she'd just speak Inuktitut for the most part with people, and so that way she killed two birds with one stone—she kept herself from being so lonely that she'd want to quit school, and she kept her language strong in her. So I really admire that, because that really shows to me what strength and wisdom she had even as a child.

More often, however, children in the English-language residential schools lost much of their ability to speak Inuktitut and, with it, connections to their families and their culture. Tracey Doherty recounts how, even though members of her family stopped using Inuktitut when they had to go to residential schools, she is trying to heal this ruptured link within her family by learning the language:

> The transmission of Inuktitut in our family stopped with my grandmother and my eldest aunt. Learning Inuktitut now is a living way to connect with my family, Inuit culture and history, and it is a creative force for reconciliation and language revitalization.

In the majority of the narratives that mention Inuktitut, the ability to speak the language or to advocate for its use is not the central focus; instead, the strengthening of relationships between people through learning Inuktitut and the celebration of a successful struggle against colonization are the inspirational aspects.

Inspiring perseverance and strength

For many narrators, the challenges some of the women faced are inspirational:

> They didn't have much, but they did a lot with what they had. They didn't have washers and dryers and electric stoves, and everything like that—imagine! ... You look back at that, and it gives you inspiration to go on and do what you needs to do with so much what we got now. (Polly Jacque about Jane Andersen)

Thinking about how the women survived their own struggles helps the narrators face their own challenges, as Joanne Voisey relates about her grandmother, Rhoda Voisey:

To me, she is a woman of great strength and courage. My grandfather passed away, and my grandmother raised her children on her own. She didn't remarry, so she had to work hard in a time when there wasn't a lot of modern conveniences, and she had to do a lot of hard work on her own. She had to provide for her children outside of the home, she had to work, as well as do everything that you'd have to do to raise a family of ten children … I feel her influence in my life. I can see it in the lives of my family and in my mother, as she goes through her own struggles and needs to persevere—I can see that strength from my grandmother in her and in her being…. I know that when I go through hard times, or I'm struggling with things, trying to raise my children, that I draw on the strength of my grandmother.

Jodie Lane describes this strength in the women of her grandmother's social circle:

They [Mary E. Andersen and Aunt Peace Andersen] have a strength that you cannot measure. A strength that comes from carrying each of your precious babies to term with little to no prenatal care and then delivering them without the comfort of pain medication or security of modern medical facilities. A strength that comes from seeing your own child on death's door and having no one but yourself to depend on to ensure that he lives. A strength that comes from doing without so that your children can have more. A strength that they did not ask for, but embraced. I long for this strength.

Jodie illustrates this strength further when she tells the story of how Mary E. Andersen managed to save her two-year-old son when he was attacked by a husky dog by sewing up his head wound, an event that later motivated her to earn her nursing certification through correspondence so that she could help others. Jodie asks herself:

> Would I have been able to be as strong as my Gram? In the face of tragedy, would I have been able to stand up and do what was needed? She did. They all did. We are here because of those strong women who were resourceful, courageous, smart, and brave. They were heroes and we must continue to honour them. Let us be resourceful and courageous and smart and brave. Let us be like them. Strong and beautiful.

Similarly, Diane Obed attributes her own ability to persevere through difficult circumstances with strength and grace to Zippie Nochasak's impact:

> Amazingly, she finds humour in true Inuk form by finding laughter and humour in some of the most challenging and tough situations. Just by modelling and radiating her own light, she's showed me how to stand and be a proud Inuk woman.

Julie Dicker relates how Sue Harris faced adversity with composure and serenity:

> When I think of my Ma, I think of her as a pillar of kindness, a pillar of truth, and a pillar of strength, because no matter what happens in her life or in her family's life, it could be a

time of celebration, it could be a time of hardships, it could be a time of triumphs, it could be times of tragedy, there could be good times, bad times, ugly times, but no matter what happens, she kind of rides the waves right on through, and comes out standing on top as if nothing happened—it's just like normal. She always keeps herself grounded, and she remains steadfast and true to everything. No matter what happens, she never sways far from her normal…. My Ma, Sue Harris, is one strong woman who never gives up.

In the face of adversity, Selma Jararuse, too, perseveres and emerges with new wisdom:

I've heard stories of her past, and the trials and triumphs that she has went through as a woman growing up in the community of Nain. She went through a lot of abuse, a lot of very negative things, but still to this day, she's very strong, she's very resilient, she's very happy-go-lucky. She has a lot of wisdom, and a lot of knowledge…. My mother is somebody that takes things that happen to her and learns from them in order to better her life and to makes her a happier person…. She don't let her past or the negative things define her. She learns from it and moves on. (Selma Jararuse by Salome Jararuse)

RELATIONSHIPS, LEADERSHIP, AND CONFRONTING COLONIALISM

The common threads that emerge from the *Daughters of Mikak* narratives illustrate a distinct style of leadership. By helping and sharing with others, looking after family and community members, teaching, being patient and humble, being on the land and speaking Inuktitut together, being outspoken, and persevering, these women improve the lives of those around them by creating supportive relationships within family networks and communities. These traits differ from the hierarchical, heroic, and individualistic style that has traditionally been considered the dominant model of leadership in North America (Archuleta 2012). The *Daughters of Mikak* stories challenge us to expand our definitions of the concept. Instead of honouring individuals who stand alone and above others, leading their people with a mix of charisma, reason, confidence, and domination, the Nunatsiavut narrators value women who create community with generosity, humility, and patience. Their composure, perseverance, and resourcefulness when they are faced with challenges are celebrated, and their refusal to assert themselves as superior or more powerful than others is regarded as commendable. They do not depend on power or coercion to influence others but model behaviours and practices that others want to emulate.

The style of leadership in these stories is accessible and inclusive. Community, relationships, and responsibility toward each other are paramount; everyone's presence and involvement are valued and encouraged. In telling their stories, the narrators achieve two ends: they celebrate the women for creating strong social networks, but they themselves strengthen relationships through expressing admiration and gratitude for and with others. This dual role in the *Daughters of Mikak* narratives creates positive energy that encourages others to share their stories. Facebook statistics describe those engaged in the project as being 77 per cent women, and, as noted above, the majority of these narrators are women. The creation of community through the project occurs mainly among women connected with Nunatsiavut, and although this is probably significant in itself, the style of leadership in the *Daughters of Mikak* project does not preclude men from displaying similar behaviour. Although this initiative asked only about women, none of the digital stories made any claims about how Inuit women and men are different or that the distinct style of leadership is exclusive to women.

The importance that the narrators place on generosity, patience, humility, and community echoes other discussions about Inuit governance, social control, and values (Briggs 1970; Pauktuutit 2006; Stern 2010). However, these stories show how Nunatsiavummiut confront ongoing colonialism. The narratives are almost universally positive and uncritical, and references to negative or difficult situations emphasize survival more than suffering. They briefly mention hardships in general terms—people "suffer," face "hard times," deal with a "tragedy," are "hungry" or "not so fortunate," or "need help"— but the narrators offer few details about the crises. Instead, they celebrate the women's reaction and ways of improving challenging situations: "[She is] always willing to help, no matter what." The social realities of Nunatsiavut can be harsh, and the impacts of years of colonialism are widespread: high rates of substance abuse, suicide, domestic abuse, accidental death, poverty, children in care, overcrowded housing, loss of language, unemployment—the list goes on. But the *Daughters of Mikak* stories and the women celebrated in them are not defined or dominated by the hardships that surround them; instead, they show how to overcome adversity by connecting with and supporting each other. Their leadership focuses on creating a strong community that endures the many processes that work to fragment it. Colonialism has attempted to destroy links between family members through forcing people into alienating experiences at residential schools and by encouraging the erosion of Indigenous languages; it threatens links between Indigenous peoples and their land through policies that remove them from their homeland, impede traditional livelihoods, and compel a town-based life; and it attacks relationships between Inuit by undermining the Indigenous governance structures and means of Inuit authority within families and communities. As Linda Tuhiwai Smith argues, "Imperialism and colonialism brought complete disorder to colonized peoples, disconnecting them from their histories, their landscapes, their languages, their social relations and their own ways of thinking, feeling, and interacting with the world. It was a process of systematic fragmentation" (2012, 29). Relationships are one of the main targets of colonization's constant assault. As this project shows, those who rebuild and strengthen social connections are honoured as leaders in Nunatsiavut society. In binding people together, they successfully challenge and confront colonialism's attempts to fragment Inuit culture and community.

Charlotte Wolfrey uses the image of the medicinal plant *Tulligunnak* (or Roseroot/Rhodiola/*Rhodiola rosea*) that grows in Labrador to symbolize Nunatsiavut women's leadership. This plant, which grows on sea cliffs and along the shore, can survive for a long time and under difficult circumstances. Specimens that have been collected and pressed in plant presses for months have put out new growth, and the roots of this plant can reach amazing proportions—they form the bulk of the plant on the surface of the rock and penetrate small cracks to create a network of support for the rest of the plant. Roots can be broken into pieces to form new plants, although a plant will die if its roots are removed. *Tulligunnak* roots are used to treat depression, fatigue, and low immunity (Mardones et al. 2014). Wolfrey sees many parallels between the patient strength of Inuit women to unite people and the endurance of *Tulligunnak*, in the ways that roots connect and anchor the plants to withstand the elements.

In choosing not to elaborate on hardships, but to celebrate the women's ability to persevere, the *Daughters of Mikak* narrators emphasize the wisdom that is gained through difficulties. The project's advisory group was adamant that participants be given the freedom to discuss both positive and negative experiences in their narratives. They steered the project from more traditional and critical approaches to research that would focus, for instance, on the challenges that Nunatsiavut women face or on the history of the women's movement in the region. Their guidance echoes what Eve Tuck (2009, 409) describes as a move from "damage-centred research" toward strength-based research. Instead of inviting Indigenous peoples to participate in research only through "speaking their pain" in order to document damage and the need for change, a "desire-based" narrative "does not deny the experience of tragedy, trauma, and pain, but positions the knowing derived from such experiences as wise" (Tuck and Yang 2014, 231). The *Daughters of Mikak* project focused on celebration and strength, illustrating the wisdom of those who create community to confront colonialism. It also portrays the richness of Nunatsiavut life and the depth of Inuit culture to provide meaningful governance structures that offer resistance and healing from social harm. As Nishnaabeg scholar Leanne Simpson argues, Indigenous renaissance and resurgence relies on "significantly re-investing in our own ways of being: regenerating our political and intellectual traditions; articulating and living our legal systems; language learning; ceremonial and spiritual pursuits; creating and using our artistic and performance-based traditions" (2011, 17–18). The *Daughters of Mikak* stories offer a Nunatsiavut-based narrative about Inuit women's leadership, and they embody the power of storytelling to re-create and inspire Indigenous resurgence, rooted firmly in Inuit values, governance practices, and leadership.

A poem by Tracey Doherty, a Memorial University education student from Nunatsiavut, beautifully conveys this idea of strong relationships. She made two digital stories for the *Daughters of Mikak* project: the first recounts the difficulties that her family endured because of her grandmother's years in residential school; the second, a poem, illustrates the power of connections, roots, and language to bind us together.

> Sikoak—thin ice through which we fell
> I touch bottom
> Roots reach me
> Yearning roots, as I have yearned
> Anânatsiaga [my grandmother], your spirit is with me
> Anânaga [my mother], your voice speaks too.

NOTES

1   The Nunatsiavut Government and Memorial University of Newfoundland developed a five-year SSHRC-funded partnership called Tradition and Transition among the Labrador Inuit that brings Inuit and non-Inuit academics and community researchers together to embark on research projects based on community ideas and interests.

2   Andrea Procter (Memorial University), with Charlotte Wolfrey, the Nunatsiavut Government's Status of Women Co-ordinator, and the AnânauKatiget Tumingit Regional Inuit Women's Association, developed a one-year initiative called *Daughters of Mikak: Celebrating Inuit Women's Leadership in Nunatsiavut.* They invited women from each community in and around Nunatsiavut to form an advisory working group; it was composed of Beverly Hunter, Hopedale; Peggy Andersen and Ashley Dicker, Nain; Joan Andersen and Tracy Ann Evans-Rice, Makkovik; Shirley Goudie, Postville; Charlotte Wolfrey, Rigolet;

Shirley Flowers, Happy Valley-Goose Bay; and Kim Campbell-McLean, North West River (executive director, AnânauKatiget Tumingit).

3 Digital stories were a good fit for Nunatsiavut, as they combine people's voices and photographs in short digital files that are easy to view with the often-limited Internet capacity in the region. Project participants were asked for their informed consent to use their names and their stories for public use.

4 The Facebook site remains the primary means of sharing the project and engaging with the public, although some of the stories have also been used for radio segments on OKâlaKatiget Society's radio station in Nain, in a *Them Days* magazine issue on Labrador women in March 2017, and in a *Newfoundland Quarterly* magazine article in December 2017.

5 According to the Nunatsiavut Tourism website, the population of Nunatsiavut in 2020 is 2,711 (https://www.tourismnunatsiavut.com/home/communities.htm).

6 We used thematic analysis to explore the narratives and to think about their social function (Katriel 2012; Riessman 2008), but, in honouring the narrators' involvement in the project, respected the integrity of their stories and tried not to objectify by over-analyzing.

REFERENCES

Archuleta, Michelle. 2012. "Approaching Leadership through Culture, Story, and Relationships." In *Living Indigenous Leadership*, edited by Carolyn Kenny and Tina Ngaroimata Fraser, 162–75. Vancouver: UBC Press.

Brantenberg, Terje. 1977. "Ethnic Commitments and Local Government in Nain, 1969–76." In *The White Arctic: Anthropological Essays on Tutelage and Ethnicity*, edited by Robert Paine, 376–410. St. John's: ISER Books.

Briggs, Jean. 1970. *Never in Anger: Portrait of an Eskimo Family*. Cambridge: Harvard University Press.

Briggs, Jean. 1974. "Eskimo Women: Makers of Men." In *Many Sisters:*

Women in Cross-Cultural Perspective, edited by Carolyn Matthiasson, 261–304. London: Free Press.

Fay, Amelia. 2014. "Big Men, Big Women, or Both? Examining the Coastal Trading System of the Eighteenth-Century Labrador Inuit." In *History and Renewal of Labrador's Inuit-Metis*, edited by John Kennedy, 75–93. St. John's: ISER Books.

Katriel, Tamar. 2012. "Analyzing the Social Life of Personal Experience Stories." In *Varieties of Narrative Analysis*, edited by James Holstein and Jaber Gubrium, 273–91. London: Sage.

Kleivan, Helge. 1966. *The Eskimos of Northeast Labrador: A History of Eskimo-White Relations, 1771–1955.* Oslo: Norse Polarinstitutt.

Mardones, Vanessa, Luise Hermanutz, and Alain Cuerrier. 2014. "The Ethnobotany and Medicinal Properties of Rhodiola (*Rhodiola rosea*) in Labrador and Potential Applications in Community-Based Nutraceutical Marketing Enterprises." Research Report. Memorial University of Newfoundland, St. John's.

McGrath, Robin. 1997. "Circumventing the Taboos: Inuit Women's Autobiographies." In *Undisciplined Women: Tradition and Culture in Canada*, edited by Pauline Greenville and Diane Tye, 223–33. Montreal: McGill-Queen's University Press.

Pauktuutit Inuit Women of Canada. 2006. *The Inuit Way: A Guide to Inuit Culture.* Ottawa: Pauktuutit.

Procter, Andrea. 2016. "Uranium and the Boundaries of Indigeneity in Nunatsiavut, Labrador." *The Extractive Industries and Society* 3: 288–96.

Riessman, Catherine Kohler. 2008. *Narrative Methods for the Human Sciences.* London: Sage.

Simpson, Leanne. 2011. *Dancing on Our Turtle's Back: Stories of Nishnaabeg Re-Creation, Resurgence, and a New Emergence.* Winnipeg: Arbeiter Ring Press.

Smith, Linda Tuhiwai. 2012. *Decolonizing Methodologies: Research and Indigenous Peoples.* 2nd ed. London: Zed Books.

Stern, Pamela. 2010. *Daily Life of the Inuit.* Westport: Greenwood Press.

Stopp, Marianne. 2009. "Eighteenth Century Labrador Inuit in England." *Arctic* 62, no. 1: 45–64.

Taylor, Garth. 1983. "The Two Worlds of Mikak: Part I." *The Beaver* 314, no. 3: 4–13.

Taylor, Garth. 1984. "The Two Worlds of Mikak: Part II." *The Beaver* 314, no. 4: 18–25.

Tuck, Eve. 2009. "Suspending Damage: A Letter to Communities." *Harvard Educational Review* 9, no. 3: 409–27.

Tuck, Eve, and K. Wayne Yang. 2014. "R-Words: Refusing Research." In *Humanizing Research: Decolonizing Qualitative Inquiry with Youth and Communities*, edited by Django Paris and Maisha Winn, 223–48. London: Sage.

Labrador Inuit Leadership—1970s to 2005*

David Lough

Over a period of thirty-five years, beginning in the early 1970s and ending with a land claim signing in 2005, the Inuit of Labrador experienced a revolutionary change. The transition from having almost no power over their own lives and future to establishing a self-government model was achieved through resilience and the contribution of committed community leaders. This was a historic period of empowerment, major organizational change, and emerging community-based leadership. It was a period in Labrador when key decisions were made which established a new narrative in the socio-economic development of the territory and set the stage for better living conditions and new hope for the Indigenous and settler residents of northern Labrador.

For Labrador Inuit the journey began by building a grounded community-based organization, then carefully, through a process of engagement, documenting the vast area of land use and unique

---

* Editor's note: This chapter is in large part a personal recollection of a process in which the author was a participant as well as an observer. While some documentation is provided to give broader information and perspective on the processes and circumstances described, this is essentially a first-hand account based on the author's intimate knowledge of the events and the people concerned, set within a historical context.

history of occupation of northern Labrador. The timing was right in Canada and in Newfoundland to obtain recognition and support as an Indigenous group. However, the key was to present a strong legal case that in fact Inuit lived in and occupied significant territory in northern Labrador for hundreds of years and that the contemporary occupants of the land were their descendants. It was an uphill battle: previous efforts to speak up had been squashed by authorities. The 1949 Terms of Union did not mention provincial Aboriginal peoples. Decisions were made by external agencies, and voices from the communities were muted. Governments treated northern Labrador as a problem area and a liability.

After Confederation, forced relocation occurred with the closure of the Inuit communities of Nutak and Hebron in the 1950s. The impact on families and their descendants has had lasting implications for northern Inuit and was a critical part of land claim discussions. The impact of children taken away to residential schools and the forced relocation of families from northern settlements remain even in the twenty-first century as the saddest period in Labrador Inuit history and has left lasting intergenerational trauma. A rich and unique Labrador Inuit culture and language and protection of their vast area of land were being threatened.

A strong desire for change brought hope in the 1970s with the emergence of a national movement for the recognition of identity and traditional rights and the empowerment of Aboriginal peoples. Governments, church, and medical authorities realized that an era of questioning and accountability was happening, and communities would need to be engaged in decision making. A frequent comment was, "the natives are getting restless." Up to this time decisions were made in boardrooms in St. John's and Ottawa with no consultation with local communities. In the early community meetings, confident voices emerged from each of the communities of northern Labrador: Willie Shiwak and Bob Palliser, Rigolet; Bill and Ted Andersen, Makkovik; George Sheppard, Postville; Garfield Flowers and Phillip Hunter, Hopedale; Amos Maggo and Sam Andersen, Nain; as well as Bill Edmunds and, regionally, young professionals like Bill Flowers and Mary Sillett. A new energy was driven by a passion for place, identity, and the well-being of the region.

Questioning the social and economic conditions with facts and passion and bringing attention to real inequities in how the region was being treated became louder. In an October 1977 policy paper, the Labrador Resources Advisory Council stated, "We are determined that we as residents of the territory will have a much larger part in seeing that the costs and benefits of resource development are more equally shared. We start by condemning the view that Labrador and the Canadian North are a chilly warehouse of resources for the urban, industrial heartland of the continent" (Flowers et al. 1977, 1).

Despite Churchill Falls generating power in 1971, the flooding of vast lands in the Labrador interior, and the Iron Ore Company of Canada and Wabush Mines mining iron ore for the giant North American steelmakers, life in coastal Labrador continued unchanged. But in the 1970s proposals were being proposed for offshore oil and gas exploration, a uranium mine was proposed in the central mineral belt near Makkovik, and development of the Lower Churchill Hydro Project was also proposed in central Labrador. Inuit were forceful in wanting to be heard. On the Labrador coast, poverty, poor housing, health care, and basic services (water, sewer, and airstrips) were critical issues presented by Labrador's emerging voices. Awareness of the conditions that Indigenous peoples faced and new community-based efforts to present the most pressing problems were finally bringing national attention to the region.

In the communities, leaders were emerging and significant challenges were being discussed, with support from Memorial University's Extension Services and community development agencies such as the Company of Young Canadians. Facilitated meetings and local community development workers hired to research and develop proposals provided the basic tools for community empowerment. At the local community level, in the early 1970s elected community councils were being established, and, for the first time, grassroots leaders offered to take responsibility for improving the lives of residents. The communities, with little infrastructure, no tax base, and no community plans, had to find the resources and expertise to begin the journey toward effective local government. Small community projects, mostly federally funded through the Department of the Secretary of State and Canada Manpower, built capacity in project development and administration to manage and implement local development.

In 1972 the community councils of the north coast began meeting annually in Hopedale, creating the Combined Councils of Northern Labrador (Snook 2005, 4). Councillors travelled by skidoo to discuss key common concerns. Resolutions on water and sewer, airstrips, marine and air transport, the fishery, caribou management, education—including bringing high schools to the coast and ending residential schools—and new resource developments, including a proposed uranium mine and offshore oil and gas exploration, were made. With access to media and articulate leadership, a case was made that the region had been neglected. This regional advocacy had some success, as politicians and senior officials listened, and a new federal-provincial funding program was created for coastal Labrador to address the core infrastructure and development needs that the councils had identified. Each year resolutions were approved by the gathering and sent to those departments and agencies with responsibility for the region.

The discontent in Labrador had resulted in the Government of Newfoundland's appointing a Royal Commission on Labrador in 1972; it delivered its final report in 1974 (Snowden 1974). The Commission made almost 300 recommendations on all issues in Labrador, including that the highest priority be given to the development of coastal Labrador through an agreement between the province and the federal Department of Regional Economic Expansion.

By the late 1970s governments were investing in badly needed community infrastructure on the coast, including potable drinking water and sewer—not an easy task in rocky, remote coastal communities. In addition, basic fisheries infrastructure to process and salt fish was fundamental to the survival of an inshore fishery on the coast. Investments were made in communications infrastructure and transportation with a new microwave system and the development of airstrips. Improvements were being made but the inequity of services that were available on the island of Newfoundland and those on the Labrador coast remained.

The authority and financial resources to improve the lives of Inuit in northern Labrador, a little-known, remote region, rested in Ottawa and St. John's, but with access to media and collective action, clear social and economic needs were being heard and a call to action ensued. The needs of each community were identified and, for the most part, the relevant government departments began to dialogue and work with the communities on solutions to the most critical issue: potable drinking water.

INUIT IDENTITY

Across Canada a movement was under way among Indigenous peoples to organize and define identity. In the early 1970s Charlie Watt, president of the Northern Quebec Inuit Association, and Tagak Curley, president of Inuit Tapirisat of Canada (ITC), both travelled separately to the north Labrador coast to encourage Labrador Inuit to organize an association. The recognition that Inuit lived on the Labrador coast and were connected to their northern relatives was fundamental. The Labrador Inuit Association (LIA), created in October 1973, was officially recognized on March 26, 1975 (Government of Newfoundland and Labrador 2015). Its creation and its ability to quickly represent the interests of northern Labrador's Inuit would soon produce changes. LIA's mandate was to promote Inuit health and communities and to advance Labrador Inuit issues with Canada and Newfoundland. With the creation of LIA, start-up funds flowed from the Government of Canada to set up a small office in Nain and to hire staff. In 2001 a formal link was established with the national organization ITC, which was renamed Inuit Tapiriit Kanatami (ITK) (Freeman 2011). Gaining recognition and access to federal funds to document land use and occupancy and to prepare the legal case was pivotal for the filing of a land claim.

Leaders emerged from the community discussions: Sam Andersen of Nain was elected the first LIA president and served from 1973 to 1974, and William (Bill) Edmunds of Makkovik served as president from 1974 to 1980. Both Andersen and Edmunds were articulate and solidly rooted in their communities and culture. In 1975 a long-serving and respected Chief Elder from Nain, Martin Martin, was made Honorary President for Life. This appointment demonstrated that traditional Elder leadership was valued and would continue, despite changing times. The story of early Inuit community leadership is only now being told in books such as Rozanne Enerson Junker's *Renatus' Kayak* (2017) and Anne Budgell's *We All Expected to Die* (2018).

It was customary for Labrador Inuit to seek the advice of Elders, who were carefully chosen for election, on important matters. How Elders were chosen and their roles in providing stability and direction in Labrador communities deserves more research. They played a critical role in ensuring that Inuit values were not lost in changing times and that consultation and collective decision making continued to guide the new Inuit-led organizations.

One of the LIA's first actions was to buy two radio telephones for communication between Nain and Makkovik. The LIA also established a newsletter, printed in Nain by Christine Dicker and Rosina Kalleo on a Gestetner copying machine. This community newsletter played an important role in getting information in Inuktitut and English to every household on the north coast. From the beginning, communication was a major issue, since the communities had no home telephones and only limited air and marine transportation services. With numerous meetings occurring and decisions to be made, it became the leaders' priority to find effective ways to keep everyone informed and to provide an opportunity for dialogue.

The detailed documenting of the land claim began in September 1975, with an agreement between LIA and the Department of Indian and Northern Affairs to undertake research to provide the evidence needed to substantiate a statement of claim. An experienced team of Inuit who were intimately familiar with traditional land use and a small group of professionals, some of whom had participated in the Mackenzie Valley Pipeline Inquiry, worked closely together to build the case. After an intense period of research and community engagement, in 1977 the LIA delivered to the Government of Canada a comprehensive land use and occupancy document: *Our Footprints Are Everywhere* (Brice-Bennett 1977). Communities and leaders had worked together, through hundreds of interviews and meetings, to define the extensive area of land and sea that was home to generations of Inuit and to create a credible presentation. Documenting land use formed the basis for filing a statement of claim with the Government of Canada. In 1978 Canada accepted the Labrador Inuit Land Claim proposal for negotiation, and in 1980 the Government of Newfoundland, at the invitation of Canada, agreed to participate in the negotiation of the Labrador Inuit Land Claim. In less than a decade, Labrador Inuit had gone from being "Eskimos" with no organization or recognition as Aboriginal peoples to negotiating a thorough case for a land claim.

Changes happened, not only at the political level. In the fall of 1977, a major education conference in Nain brought together, for the first time, community members, educators, and the provincial minister of Education (Memorial University of Newfoundland 1977). This gathering was fundamental to delivering high school programs to all coastal communities; establishing a new native-teacher education program; introducing Inuktitut, Inuit history, and traditional skills-based curricula; and providing adult-education programs. Beatrice Watts, originally from Nain, who was working with the Labrador East Integrated School Board, was a spokesperson for Inuit education at the conference; her career for twenty-five years thereafter, as a key staff person with the Labrador East Integrated School Board, was devoted to preserving and restoring the Inuktitut language and the Labrador dialect. She developed a teacher-education program which finally brought Inuit teachers into the schools to promote cultural survival. Watts was awarded an Honorary Doctorate by Memorial University in 1992, and in 2005 a boardroom was named in her honour at Memorial's Bruneau Centre for Research and Innovation (Memorial University 2005). The opportunities for education and a solid grounding in Inuit culture enjoyed by generations of new Inuit leaders in Labrador was attributable in no small part to Beatrice Watts's leadership in education from the 1970s to her death in 2004.

A key priority for the LIA, from the beginning, was the protection and promotion of the Labrador Inuit language and culture. In 1981 the Torngâsok Cultural Centre was established in Nain as a separate entity to focus solely on culture and language. Its first priority was preserving and promoting the Labrador dialect; Rose Pamak began that task, which continues in 2020. Policies were developed around the repatriation of human remains, protecting special places such as Hebron, archaeology assessments, and the protection of artifacts. Research partners included the Arctic Studies Center at the Smithsonian Institution, Bowdoin College in Maine, and Memorial University, all of which contributed to building a knowledge base and conducting research on the span of Labrador Inuit history.

Torngâsok Cultural Centre leaders Gary Baikie and Catharyn Andersen worked passionately to protect and present Labrador's rich Inuit culture. The original dream was that the centre would showcase the importance of culture to Inuit. The school building that housed it was destroyed by fire in 2005 (CBC News 2005), and a new centre, in its own new building, was planned to assume its role. In June 2016, the Government of Canada announced that it would contribute funding and other support, from four federal departments and agencies, to the Nunatsiavut Government's construction of the Illusuak Cultural Centre in Nain (Government of Canada 2016). Celebrating Labrador Inuit culture and values and ensuring that youth were immersed in them were priorities for the new institution. In the words of Johannes Lampe, the president of Nunatsiavut: "this cultural centre is being built *by* Labrador Inuit, *for* Labrador Inuit, to tell stories *about* Labrador Inuit.... Illusuak will give our culture a home, bringing generations together to share experiences and expertise. This centre will honour our culture, encouraging all Labrador Inuit to continue our traditions ... for future generations" (Government of Canada 2016). The new Centre opened in November 2019.

The LIA also recognized that communication challenges in remote communities were a major problem (Flowers et al. 1977). In 1982, with support from the federal Department of Secretary of State, a new communications network, the OKâlaKatiget (OK) Society, was incorporated to preserve and promote the cultural identity of Labrador Inuit (OKâlaKatiget Society 2017). Language programming, public awareness, and discussion of crucial issues were central to the organization's mandate. The OK Society played a vital role in information distribution and Inuktitut language promotion, at the same time creating a comprehensive documentary archive of stories and development from each community in video, audio, and print formats. William Kalleo's leadership as a community journalist and cultural champion quickly made the OK Society a popular and essential part of community life.

Organizational development, with all Inuit regions in Canada working together, including Labrador Inuit, as key participants, occurred at the national level. For example, in 1984 Pauktuutit, the Inuit Women's Association of Canada, was founded; as of 2020, it continues to work at advancing the issues of Inuit women and children (Pauktuutit 2019).

In 1980 the LIA elected Fran (Frieda) Williams, originally from Hopedale, as president. Williams, the first woman president, served in this capacity until 1984. She had trained as a registered nurse in St. John's and had practiced in North West River before joining the Company of Young Canadians on a community development project and later adult-education initiatives on the north coast. Under her leadership, the Torngâsok Cultural Centre, the OKâlaKatiget Society, and Labrador's contribution to Pauktuutit developed; she also led a focus on education and programmes to support youth.

The cultural economy of Labrador communities was rich in traditional art but had not benefited from major Inuit art initiatives in the same way as the rest of the Canadian North. In 1987 the Inuit Art Foundation was established (Inuit Art Foundation 2019) and quickly profiled Labrador Inuit artists. Gilbert Hay of Nain was an early leader in the Foundation's recognition of the uniqueness and diverse forms of Labrador Inuit crafts. A craft shop was established in Nain, and efforts were made through a Memorial University Artist-in-Residence Programme to establish a printmaking shop there.

While major economic projects were being debated in other parts of Canada—for example, the Mackenzie Valley Pipeline Inquiry in the Northwest Territories—comparably large resource development projects were being proposed in Labrador. Although the 1970s were a decade of intense political and cultural identity activity in Labrador, careful technical analysis and input into large-scale development projects were needed. The community-based Labrador leaders, who were still in the early stages of building effective organizations, were now required to address environmental and social impact concerns on large-scale development proposals. These included the Lower Churchill Hydro Project, the Brinex uranium mine proposed near Makkovik, and offshore oil and gas development by international exploration companies along the central and north Labrador coast. Although all three projects were ultimately shelved, they did provide an opportunity for leaders and communities to learn how to deal with long-term development proposals and present informed critiques to semi-judicial assessment panels.

In all the regions of Labrador, non-renewable resource management issues and major new proposed developments were a community concern, especially with Labrador's Indigenous leaders. The province, which had initiated the Lower Churchill Hydro Project at Gull Island on the Churchill River in central Labrador, started work on the crossing to Newfoundland at the Strait of Belle Isle. After an environmental assessment and the beginning of construction, the project was halted in 1976 due to a lack of sales contracts for the power and financial problems.

An environmental assessment was also started on a uranium mine near Postville and Makkovik by Brinex, a subsidiary of BRINCO, the developer of the Churchill Falls Power Project. However, Brinex postponed its application to proceed in mid-1977 because of the declining price for uranium. The two developments which required major attention were put on hold, giving Labrador leaders time to concentrate on community and organizational development.

In the 1970s exploratory drilling for oil and gas was also under way in the Labrador Sea off Hopedale; the wildcat wells produced significant gas reserves but no oil. Ocean protection and management and community concern to protect fish stocks were discussed by all the local fisheries committees and documented in policy papers by the Labrador Resources Advisory Council. By the early 1980s the companies shifted their interest from Labrador to the Grand Banks, where significant oil was showing in the drilling programs. Meanwhile, in the coastal communities, the future of the fishery was the major concern and efforts began to create locally controlled fishing entities to manage resource allocations, harvesting, and processing. Coastal Labrador fishermen were struggling and the communities received limited services or support. In the fishery the issue of adjacency and the rights of small-boat inshore fishermen were being presented by articulate local leaders. Bill Edmunds, LIA president, was a central persuasive leader. He had a commanding presence, a sense of humour, and the ability to engage in discussions on key issues and he was not intimidated by business or government leaders. He was able to build relationships with new allies nationally and in Labrador who believed that the time had come to establish communities' right to have a say in the management of resources near them.

RESOURCE ISSUES

In response to the growing concern about resource exploitation, in January 1976 the Labrador Resources Advisory Council was created to develop policies to ensure that Labrador resources would be managed with input from the communities directly affected. The new council, made up of representatives from all regions of Labrador, worked to connect with all stakeholder groups in Labrador to formulate policy positions on essential issues which impacted the communities. In December 1978 the Labrador Resources Advisory Council, following a year of consultation, delivered a detailed report, "Community Priorities for Development in Labrador," to the federal and provincial governments (Labrador Resources Advisory Council 1978). It formed the basis of a special agreement for coastal Labrador through funding from the federal Department of Regional Economic Expansion. The agreement addressed the lack of basic infrastructure, including water and sewer, airstrips, fish processing, schools, and transportation. Labrador Inuit leaders were pivotal in this council.

For the Labrador Inuit a priority for economic development was the struggling inshore fishery on the north coast. While arctic char was abundant in the north, it had to be preserved in brine, as did salmon farther south, and collection and market distribution were expensive. The once lucrative cod stocks were being depleted and concern was expressed about the negative impacts of trawlers offshore and the potential effects and risks of oil and gas exploration.

A significant accomplishment of the Labrador Resources Advisory Council was in working with the federal Department of Fisheries. In February 1977 an important meeting in Labrador resulted in a decision, in June 1978, by the federal minister Romeo Leblanc and his director general Len Cowley to reserve for Labrador three of the eleven new offshore shrimp licences. Among community leaders at this historic fisheries meeting were Henry John Williams, Bill Edmunds, Toby Andersen, Mary Sillett, Bill Flowers, Tim McNeil, Amos Maggo, Violet Ford, Bertha Kairtok, and Hilda Lyall. Each represented a community or organization and all were skilled ambassadors for change, asking informed questions and demonstrating a passion for place, which was understood by the federal minister, who was of Acadian ancestry. Following the meeting with the federal minister, a Fishery Policy Emergency Committee (FPEC) was established. It included representatives of the six northern Labrador communities, the LIA, and the Labrador Resources Advisory Council. It negotiated the takeover from the province's Labrador Services Division of the operation of fish plants at Nain and Makkovik and the establishment of a regional co-operative for the Labrador Inuit shrimp licence and the management of fisheries infrastructure in northern Labrador. In 1981 the Torngat Fish Producers Co-operative was established (Torngat Fish Producers Co-operative 2019) and the shrimp licence that had been held in trust for northern Labrador was given to the new Co-op (Labrador Morning 2014). With no offshore vessel, Torngat Co-op contracted offshore shrimp harvesters to catch its quota in return for a portion of the revenue. This revenue source supported inshore fishery development activities on the coast.

In southern Labrador in 1978 the Labrador Fisherman's Union Shrimp Company was established as a co-operative and allocated two of the offshore shrimp licences (Roberts 2018). Both organizations, Torngat Fisheries and the Labrador Shrimp Company, operate in 2020 with significant revenues flowing back to the communities from the historic 1978 offshore shrimp licence allocation.

COMMUNITY DEVELOPMENT

By the late 1970s, the focus of the leaders had shifted to community-based projects designed to improve the well-being of the communities and to build capacity in the journey to a land claim, and ultimately to self-government. In the 1980s the focus was on Labrador Inuit community and social issues and the implementation of federal funding, which was in place for the new Indigenous organizations and allowed for investments in badly needed community improvements. Among the key infrastructure investments was the building of airstrips in each community, giving improved access to health care and fresh food. William Andersen served as LIA president from 1984 to 1990; Tony Andersen and Joe Dicker as vice-presidents and acting president in the late 1980s and early 1990s. Their leadership focused on improving the well-being of residents on the north coast. Sam Andersen, LIA's first president, returned to the presidency twenty years later, in 1994/1995. He was a positive and popular leader at the community level, especially with his fluency in Inuktitut and skill as a translator. By the end of the 1980s community-level improvements were slowly beginning. In all the communities, water and sewer systems were in place, housing problems were being addressed through the Inuit-controlled Torngat Regional Housing Authority (Barker 2016; Government of Newfoundland and Labrador 1998), and new schools were being built.

Lough_

FINAL JOURNEY TO A LAND CLAIM

In November 1990, twelve years after the claim was accepted for negotiation, the governments of Newfoundland and Canada satisfied the first stage of the land claim process by signing a framework agreement with the LIA that set out the process and subjects for negotiation (Nunatsiavut Government 2019). Negotiations proceeded slowly and, in 1993, there was an exchange of proposals with respective positions on all subjects. Meanwhile, in 1992, Parks Canada, the LIA, and the province announced a joint public study to assess the feasibility of creating a national park in the Torngat Mountains. The resulting report by Parks Canada in 1996 concluded that such a park was feasible (Government of Newfoundland and Labrador 2005). Identifying the importance of the Torngat Mountains for Labrador Inuit was a key issue.

In November 1996 the Royal Commission on Aboriginal Peoples concluded that a complete restructuring of the relationship between Aboriginal and non-Aboriginal peoples in Canada was needed (Dussault et al. 1996). Mary Sillett of Hopedale, who had been president of the National Inuit Women's organization and a vice-president of ITK, was the Commission's only Inuit member. The timing of the Royal Commission report worked favourably for advancing the Labrador land claim in Ottawa, and Sillett helped ensure that Labrador Inuit issues were included in the recommendations.

A development which gave the Labrador Inuit a strong negotiating position was the nickel discovery in Voisey's Bay, 30 kilometres south of Nain, in September 1993 (Kerr 2003). Suddenly, international mining and stock market attention focused on this remote region. An exploration boom resulted: the nickel, copper, and cobalt discovery was the biggest discovery in Canada in decades. At the peak, the Nain airstrip had more flight activity in a day than Halifax

International Airport. At one point more than twenty helicopters overnighted in Nain. International attention from business and governments was, for the first time, focused on northern Labrador. There was pressure to move ahead quickly with a development agreement to mine this vast rich open-pit deposit, but the outstanding land claim needed to be resolved. At this critical time William Barbour, a forceful and articulate Inuit leader from Nain, became LIA president, in 1995. His knowledge of the land claim area and his skills as a team player and communicator were critical factors in making a deal. He credits Nain elders Martin Martin and Jerry Sillett, from the 1960s and 1970s, for giving him the foundation of traditional Inuit values and leadership.

Labrador Inuit took the firm position that a mine development at Voisey's Bay could not proceed prior to reaching an agreement in principle on the Labrador Inuit land claim. In July 1996 Newfoundland premier Brian Tobin, LIA president William Barbour, and Ron Irwin, federal minister of Indian Affairs and Northern Development, agreed to fast-track negotiations. With Barbour was a negotiating team of community representatives and advisors and expert staff, including Veryan Haysom, Judy Rowell, and Isabelle Pain. Politically, it was Barbour, with his engaging yet firm style, who ultimately became the deal maker. He worked closely with his team but also one-to-one with three premiers—Clyde Wells, Brian Tobin, and Roger Grimes—as well as federal ministers Ron Irwin, Jane Stewart, and Robert Nault. The Labrador Inuit negotiating team spent months in St. John's, away from family and their communities. The team engaged Elders whose expert knowledge of the land clearly aligned with the research on land use. Elected LIA officials were also forceful and passionate about the challenges faced in the communities and the need for improved services, as well as hope and opportunities for Inuit youth.

The team maintained a dialogue with all communities while major items were being negotiated, which had positive consequences when it came to a ratification vote.

The Labrador Inuit team gained respect from both federal and provincial governments for their commitment to the process of detailed negotiation and their fact-based approach. Establishing a division between Labrador-Inuit-owned lands and settlement-area lands and the question of shared jurisdictions were intense, and difficult decisions were needed. Despite the desire to settle, the Inuit negotiating team remained firm on the most important issues, including impact benefit agreements. Premiers Clyde Wells and Brian Tobin were frustrated by Inuit unwillingness to come to a quick settlement, as a deal with INCO for Voisey's Bay was contingent on a successful land claim. The priority for the Newfoundland government was the creation of ore-processing jobs on the island of Newfoundland, and Premier Grimes reached a deal with INCO to have Voisey's Bay ore processed at a new smelter to be built on the Avalon Peninsula.

In late October 1997, the three parties reached the basis for an agreement in principle, which began the process of lawyers, financial experts, and land claims specialists working on the detailed text for ratification. In 1999 the agreement in principle was initialed by the chief negotiators and recommended to their respective parties for ratification (Government of Newfoundland and Labrador 1999). On May 26, 2004, the Labrador Inuit ratified the agreement with the support of 76.4 per cent of eligible voters with an 86 per cent voter turnout (Government of Newfoundland and Labrador 2004). The earlier experience of organizing and addressing community needs gave the leaders the skills to face a team of negotiators and a rigorous process of time commitment, travel, and focus on detailed clauses but also the continued connection and support of the communities.

Ultimately, it was Barbour and Grimes who signed the critical agreement in principle. Grimes, an experienced negotiator, built a relationship of respect with Barbour, setting the stage for the final ratification of the claim in 2004.

The stage was set for the historic signing of the Labrador Inuit claim. On January 22, 2005, the Labrador Inuit land claim was signed in Nain with LIA president William Andersen signing for Labrador Inuit, Premier Danny Williams for the province, and Andy Scott, minister of Indian Affairs and Northern Development, for the Government of Canada. The agreement, a modern-day treaty, was the first of its kind in Atlantic Canada: It set out details of land ownership, resource sharing, and self-governance (Government of Newfoundland and Labrador 2018). Included at the signing ceremony was the apology and compensation for those forced to relocate from Nutak in 1956 and Hebron in 1959. The Labrador Inuit negotiating team had remained firm that this difficult period had to be addressed in the settlement—that Hebron would be designated a special historic place and a national park created: the Torngat Mountains National Park. Inuit leaders gifted back to Canada approximately 9,600 square kilometres of land, with a unique agreement for Inuit co-management of the park. As it turned out, the Government of Canada appointees were all Inuit, resulting in a total Inuit co-management board.

CONCLUSION

This chapter provides highlights of a crucial period in the history of Labrador Inuit. The details of the creation of the LIA and the long journey for recognition of their claim to northern Labrador deserve thorough research and analysis. The major contributions of the many

Labrador Inuit leaders and advisors who worked diligently on the long land claim journey, the team that forged the fine details and ultimately the Labrador Inuit community that voted in favour need to be presented for the benefit of future generations. The exemplary community leadership resulted in the creation of a modern-day treaty, the territory of Nunatsiavut, and a unique form of Indigenous self-government in Canada. For Labrador Inuit, December 1, 2005, was the end of one historic chapter and the beginning of another. The ultimate evaluation of what was achieved will be how the well-being of Labrador Inuit and a distinct Inuit culture in northern Labrador has improved.

REFERENCES

Barker, Jacob. 2016. "After 20 Months in Tent, Nain Man Moves into New House." CBC *Here and Now*: "Out of the Cold," May 24, 2016. https://www.cbc.ca/news/canada/newfoundland-labrador/nain-man-gets-new-house-after-20-months-in-tent-1.3591939.

Brice-Bennett, Carol. 1977. *Our Footprints Are Everywhere: Inuit Land Use and Occupancy in Labrador.* Nain: Labrador Inuit Association.

Budgell, Anne. 2018. *We All Expected to Die.* St. John's: ISER Books.

Enerson Junker, Rozanne. 2017. *Renatus' Kayak.* Gatineau, QC: Polar Horizons Inc.

CBC News. 2005. "Historical Items Destroyed in Nain Fire." March 8, 2005. https://www.cbc.ca/news/canada/newfoundland-labrador/historical-items-destroyed-in-nain-fire-1.531672.

Dussault, René, Georges Erasmus, Paul L. A. H. Chartrand, J. Peter Meekison, Viola Robinson, Mary Sillett, and Bertha Wilson. 1996. *Report of the Royal Commission on Aboriginal Peoples, Volume 2: Restructuring the Relationship.* Library and Archives Canada. Updated November 2, 2016. https://www.bac-lac.gc.ca/eng/discover/aboriginal-heritage/royal-commission-aboriginal-peoples/Pages/final-report.aspx.

Flowers, William, Arthur Fowler, Lawrence Jackson, David Lough, and Nigel Markham. 1977. *As If People Mattered.* Happy Valley-Goose Bay: Labrador Resources Advisory Council.

Freeman, Minnie Aodla. 2011. "Inuit Tapiriit Kanatami (ITK)." In *The Canadian Encyclopedia. Historica Canada.* Published June 27, 2011; last modified March 21, 2018. https://www.thecanadianencyclopedia. ca/en/article/inuit-tapiriit-kanatami-itk.

Government of Canada. 2016. "Illusuak Cultural Centre Will Celebrate the Culture and Heritage of Labrador Inuit." Government of Canada, news release, June 17, 2016. https://www.canada.ca/en/canadian-heritage/ news/2016/06/illusuak-cultural-centre-will-celebrate-the-culture-and-heritage-of-labrador-inuit.html.

Government of Newfoundland and Labrador. 1998. "NLHC Sells Houses to Torngat Regional Housing Association." Government of Newfoundland and Labrador, Municipal and Provincial Affairs, news release, November 3, 1998. https://www.releases.gov.nl.ca/releases/1998/NLHC/ 1103n01.htm.

Government of Newfoundland and Labrador. 1999. "Labrador Inuit Land Claims Agreement in Principle Initialled." Government of Newfoundland and Labrador, Executive Council, news release, May 10, 1999. https://www.releases.gov.nl.ca/releases/1999/exec/0510n01.htm.

Government of Newfoundland and Labrador. 2004. "Premier Announces Ratification of Labrador Inuit Land Claims Agreement Act." Government of Newfoundland and Labrador, Labrador and Aboriginal Affairs, news release, December 6, 2004. https://www.releases.gov.nl.ca/releases/ 2004/laa/1206n02.htm.

Government of Newfoundland and Labrador. 2005."Backgrounder: Torngat Mountains National Park Reserve of Canada." Government of Newfoundland and Labrador, news release, n.d. Accessed June 4, 2019. https://www.releases.gov.nl.ca/releases/2005/exec/0122n02back1.htm.

Government of Newfoundland and Labrador. 2015. "Recognizing the Contributions of Labrador Inuit." Government of Newfoundland and

Labrador, Executive Council, news release, March 26, 2015. https://www.releases.gov.nl.ca/releases/2015/exec/0326n09.aspx.

Government of Newfoundland and Labrador. 2018. "An Act to Ratify and Give the Force of Law to the Labrador Inuit Land Claims Agreement." Statutes of Newfoundland 2004, Chapter L-3.1; amended 2012. Queen's Printer, St. John's. https://www.assembly.nl.ca/legislation/sr/statutes/l03-1.htm#1_.

Inuit Art Foundation. 2019. "Welcome to the Inuit Art Foundation." Accessed May 28, 2019. https://www.inuitartfoundation.org.

Kerr, A. 2003. "Voisey's Bay and the Nickel Potential of Labrador: A Summary for the Nonspecialist." *Current Research*: 231–39. Newfoundland Department of Mines and Energy, Geological Survey, Report 03-1.

Labrador Morning. 2014. "The Torngat Fish Producers Co-op." *Labrador Morning* Season 2014, Episode 300192351, November 24, 2014. https://www.cbc.ca/player/play/2608611619.

Labrador Resources Advisory Council. 1978. *Community Priorities for Development in Labrador.* Happy Valley: Labrador Resources Advisory Council.

Memorial University. 1977. *Labrador Inuit Education Conference, Nain, Labrador, October 31 to November 4, 1977.* St. John's: Memorial University of Newfoundland, Extension Service.

Memorial University. 2005. "Centre Boardroom Named in Honour of Labrador Scholar." Memorial University, news release, September 20, 2005. http://today.mun.ca/news.php?news_id=1452.

Nunatsiavut Government. 2019. "The Path to Self-Government: How We Got to Where We Are Today." Accessed June 4, 2019. https://www.nunatsiavut.com/government/the-path-to-self-government/.

OKâlaKatiget Society. 2017. "OKâlaKatiget Society." Accessed May 24, 2019. http://www.oksociety.com.

Pauktuutit. 2019. *Pauktuutit. Inuit Women of Canada.* April 26, 2019. www.pauktuutit.ca.

Roberts, Stephen. 2018. "Labrador Fishermen's Union Shrimp Company

Marks a Milestone." *The Packet*, December 6, 2018. https://www.thepacket.ca/business/labrador-fishermens-union-shrimp-company-marks-a-milestone-265781/.

Snook, Jamie. 2005. *Labrador Organized into a Knot? History of the Combined Councils of Labrador: The Seventies, Eighties, Nineties and Twenty-First Century.* Thesis Paper, Local Economic Development Diploma Program, University of Waterloo.

Snowden, D. 1974. *Report of the Royal Commission on Labrador.* St. John's: Government of Newfoundland.

Torngat Fish Producers Co-operative. 2019. "About Our Happy Valley-Goose Bay Fish Market and Co-operative." Accessed June 4, 2019. https://www.torngatfishcoop.com/about.

PART II: SELF-DETERMINATION AND GOVERNANCE

The Nunavut Land Claims Agreement: A Modern Treaty*

Bruce Uviluq

This chapter is about the history of modern treaties between the Government of Canada and Indigenous groups, with a focus on the Nunavut Land Claims Agreement (NLCA) of 1993. It will cover the negotiation and implementation of the agreement and will explore how this and other treaties have molded the modern process of treaty-making in Canada.

To get a complete picture of modern treaties, it will be helpful to understand some of the history and how we got where we are today. Historically, modern treaties are to a great extent based on one shared theme: resources. The hard truth is that if the resources were not on Indigenous peoples' lands, we probably would not have treaties today. And it was only through litigation and protests that modern treaties as we know them evolved. A few examples illustrate this.

Alaska was granted statehood in the United States in 1959, and the Alaska Statehood Act authorized the state to select 100 million acres (roughly 405,000 square kilometres) of federally administered

*   Editor's Note: This chapter has been edited and re-written from the PowerPoint presentation delivered by the author at the 2016 Inuit Studies Conference, with the addition of extra material based on questions from the audience.

land as a form of economic support for the state. Although lands to which Alaska Natives held rights or title were exempted, the state government considered that lands used by Alaska Natives only for "subsistence" were available for selection. With the discovery of oil on Alaska's North Slope in the early 1960s, lands in that area quickly became a matter of contention, leading to lengthy challenges to state land selections and eventually to a federally imposed land freeze. The ultimate resolution was the Alaska Native Claims Settlement of 1971, which was instrumental in changing the orientation toward the settlement of Aboriginal rights and title. Through the settlement, roughly 10 per cent of the state, both surface and subsurface, was transferred to twelve Alaska Native regional corporations and 172 village, share-based corporations. In addition, approximately $962.5 million was paid to regional corporations from congressional appropriations and through royalty shares. This was a very big shift in the relations between government and Indigenous people, and it was noticed in Canada. After that agreement there was a shift from reserve-type treaties to modern comprehensive claims. Several Aboriginal groups in Canada sent representatives to Alaska to learn about this settlement.

In Canada, the first comprehensive land settlement agreement was the James Bay and Northern Quebec Agreement (JBNQA) of 1975, negotiated between the governments of Canada and Quebec, the James Bay Cree, the Inuit of northern Quebec, and later the Naskapi First Nations (see Craik and Price 2015). It was the culmination of four years of negotiation and litigation following the joint announcement by Hydro-Quebec and the Quebec government, of the James Bay Project, a massive hydroelectric power generation scheme involving a series of dams, reservoirs, and water diversions. Under the agreement, Aboriginal people negotiated specific rights to various categories of lands, amounting to over 1 million square kilometres (roughly two-thirds of the surface area of Quebec), and also received monetary compensation. Significant outcomes of this agreement included the designation of huge areas of territory for the exclusive use of Aboriginal people for traditional hunting and harvesting, a minimal family income plan for wildlife harvesting, the right to education in Indigenous languages as well as English and French, and the establishment of a corporation to encourage Aboriginal economic development.

The Inuvialuit Final Agreement, signed in 1984 after ten years of negotiations, was the first comprehensive land claim agreement in Canada north of the 60th parallel. Like the JBNQA, it saw the Inuvialuit give up certain exclusive rights to a large portion of their claimed ancestral lands in exchange for other guaranteed rights, about 91,000 square kilometres of territory, and financial considerations. In this case, the triggering issue was the discovery of oil and gas resources in the Beaufort Sea, with the consequent need to access Inuvialuit coastal and marine hunting areas, and the potential for environmental and cultural disruption.

In all of these cases, in return for guaranteeing a variety of Aboriginal rights and usage for large areas of territory, the governments in question came away with the secure right to promote resource development in significant portions of the areas that were contested or under negotiation. Government-guaranteed rights in these modern treaties generally deal with land ownership, cash compensation, land-use rights, wildlife management, harvesting rights, self-governance, and other matters. Significant differences between treaties emerge as a result of a variety of factors, including the size of the area claimed as traditional territory and the number of inhabitants or potential beneficiaries.

NUNAVUT LAND CLAIMS AGREEMENT (NLCA)

The NLCA, covering 20 per cent of Canada's land mass and 60 per cent of its coastline, was first tabled by the federal government in 1976, and was finally signed by Prime Minister Brian Mulroney on May 25, 1993. Inuit were represented in the negotiations and the agreement by the Tungavik Federation of Nunavut, later Nunavut Tunngavik Incorporated (NTI, ᓄᓇᕗᑦ ᑐᖓᕕᒃ). Like other such treaties, the NLCA is constitutionally protected, meaning that treaty rights take precedence over other statutes. Part of the impetus for the Nunavut land claim was the increasing pressure for development of the vast mineral, oil, and gas potential in Nunavut, with the obvious threat of extensive disruption to the environment and to Inuit social and cultural well-being. In the absence of an agreement and guaranteed Inuit rights, it was feared that development would be allowed to proceed without adequate controls or oversight.

The NLCA created both the new territory of Nunavut and the Government of Nunavut that represents all the citizens of the territory. This was agreed at a meeting in 1991 between the Tungavik Federation of Nunavut and the minister of Indian Affairs and Northern Development. It is worth noting that the federal government's agreement to create the territory of Nunavut came a year after the Oka Crisis, providing the government with a much-needed political "good news" story after the events of the previous year. NTI continues as the legal representative of the Nunavut's Inuit residents, about 80 per cent of the population, in treaty rights and all NLCA-related matters. The NLCA established clear rules of ownership and control over land and resources in Nunavut. As the signatory of the land claim on behalf of Inuit, the NTI mandate is to promote Inuit economic, social, and cultural well-being by ensuring that the agreement is fully implemented and that the signing parties live up to their obligations.

This is critically important, because the rights specified in the NLCA represent what the Inuit negotiated for in exchange for giving up their Aboriginal title.

Perhaps the most significant item gained by the Inuit under the NLCA is Article 4, which provides for the establishment of a new Canadian territory of Nunavut, "with its own Legislative assembly and public government, separate from the Government of the remainder of the Northwest Territories" (Government of Nunavut n.d., 23). The territory of Nunavut was officially created on April 1, 1999. The NLCA also designated 356,000 square kilometres as "Inuit Owned Lands" (Articles 17–19) to "promote economic self-sufficiency of Inuit through time, in a manner consistent with Inuit social and cultural needs and aspirations" (139–59).

The agreement established Institutions of Public Government (IPG), the main co-management bodies that are half Inuit and half government appointments. These include the Nunavut Wildlife Management Board to deal with wildlife issues and quotas, and the Nunavut Planning Commission to oversee land-use planning. NLCA also established Inuit Impact Benefit Agreements (IIBA), of which there are two kinds. IIBAs for protected areas (Articles 8 and 9) are negotiated between Inuit and government for the establishment of such protected areas as national and territorial parks, bird sanctuaries, and heritage areas, etc. (Government of Nunavut n.d., 69–85). IIBAs for major developments (Article 26) are negotiated between Inuit and proponents of major developments (205–10) and set out parameters for negotiations regarding "any matter connected with the Major Development Project that could have a detrimental impact in Inuit or that could reasonably confer a benefit on Inuit" (205). As of 2020, there are two such agreements in place: the Meadowbank Goldmine in Baker Lake and the Baffinland Iron Ore Mine near Pond Inlet.

NLCA Articles 23 and 24 set out undertakings by the Government of Canada regarding employment of Nunavut Inuit within the Federal Public Service and support for Inuit contractors bidding on government contracts (Government of Nunavut n.d., 191–201). The objective of Article 23 is "to increase Inuit participation in government employment in the Nunavut Settlement Area to a representative level," in pursuit of which aim the Government of Canada undertakes, among other measures, to "cooperate in the development and implementation of employment and training" (192). Article 24 "provide[s] reasonable support and assistance to Inuit firms ... to enable them to compete for government contracts ... [and] ... to develop, implement or maintain procurement policies respecting Inuit firms for all Government of Canada contracts required in support of its activities in the Nunavut Settlement Area" (198). Obviously, these provisions are crucial in ensuring that Inuit and Inuit firms have the capacity and opportunity to participate in, benefit from, and control the economic future of Nunavut.

In addition to the above benefits, under the NLCA the Inuit of Nunavut received $1.142 billion in capital transfers. Canada's signing the NLCA secured clear and certain title to 20 per cent of the land mass and natural resources of Canada, as opposed to having to negotiate such rights piecemeal. In addition, it obtained guarantees of a share of the royalties from major economic developments in Nunavut.

IMPLEMENTATION CHALLENGES

In spite of the good intentions and many innovative benefits of the NLCA, its implementation was far from smooth. Part of the problem was a difference of perspective and expectations between Inuit and government. From the Inuit point of view, the relationship formed by signing the agreement was just beginning. The government, however, had secured what it wanted by signing, and from its point of view, it was all done.

By 2006, the process of implementing the NLCA and the state of Nunavut and its inhabitants had reached a crisis stage (Berger 2006). The report of the Berger Enquiry identified deficiencies in collegial implementation of the NLCA, as well as major issues with Inuit education, health, and housing. It noted in addition a marked lack of progress toward a representative Inuit public sector workforce. In the face of a perceived lack of response to the Berger Report by the Government of Canada, in 2016 NTI, representing the Nunavut Inuit, initiated a court action against the Crown for breach of its contractual duties under the NLCA, seeking $1 billion in damages. This resulted in a summary judgment in 2012 in favour of NTI for $14.8 million, which the Government of Canada appealed in 2014. With a trial date set for 2015, NTI and the Government of Canada reached an out-of-court settlement for $255.5 million and agreed to a new dispute resolution mechanism involving arbitration.

GOING FORWARD

The legacy of the Nunavut-Canada lawsuit has overall been positive. The Government of Canada is now [in 2020] working with NTI to implement the NLCA. More widely, Canada is working collaboratively with Aboriginal groups on other modern treaties. Among the positive outcomes are a Cabinet policy regarding the negotiation and implementation of modern treaties, the establishment of a Modern Treaty Implementation Office, and the creation of an Oversight Committee chaired at the deputy minister level.

Everyone—both Inuit and government—wins when agreements

are followed. These recent positive developments are helping us to advance the NTI mission: to foster Inuit economic, social, and cultural well-being through implementation of the NLCA.

REFERENCES

Berger, Thomas R. 2006. Conciliator's Final Report: Nunavut Land Claims Agreement Implementation Planning Contract Negotiations for the Second Planning Period. Report to the Minister of Indian Affairs and Northern Development. Accessed August 23, 2018 (site discontinued). https://www.aadnc-aandc.gc.ca/eng/1100100030982/1100100030985.

Craik, Brian, and John A. Price. 2015. "James Bay and Northern Quebec Agreement." *The Canadian Encyclopedia*. First published 2011, revised 2019. https://www.thecanadianencyclopedia.ca/en/article/james-bay-and-northern-quebec-agreement/.

Government of Nunavut. n.d. "Agreement between the Inuit of the Nunavut Settlement Area and Her Majesty the Queen in Right of Canada." Accessed August 22, 2018. https://www.gov.nu.ca/sites/default/files/Nunavut_Land_Claims_Agreement.pdf.

Institutional Design and Inuit Governance: Nunatsiavut and Nunavut Compared

Graham White and Christopher Alcantara

Although settled comprehensive land claim agreements are in place in all four regions of Inuit Nunangat, governance arrangements in them vary in fundamental ways (Wilson, Alcantara, and Rodon 2020). In the Inuvialuit Settlement Region, the Government of the Northwest Territories has primary responsibility for the provision of programmes and services, with Inuit interests represented primarily by two land claims organizations, the Inuvialuit Regional Corporation and the Inuvialuit Game Council. In Nunavik, three regional government bodies govern alongside an Inuit land claims organization, the Makivik Corporation. As an Indigenous self-government, the Nunatsiavut Government restricts certain services and political rights to Inuit beneficiaries only. No Inuit land claims corporation represents Inuit interests. Finally, in Nunavut, Inuit chose to create a new territory with a "public" government in which services are provided to all residents, regardless of their status under the claim; Inuit interests, however, are protected and promoted by a land claims corporation, Nunavut Tunngavik Incorporated (NTI).

Despite these differences, the four regions of Inuit Nunangat share important goals and aspirations. Each desires government committed to promoting representation, inclusiveness, responsiveness, and public participation, yet the ways in which their governments enact these democratic principles vary considerably. One of the starkest contrasts between the regions is that between the Inuit self-government regime in Nunatsiavut and the Inuit-dominated public government of Nunavut.

At first glance, the notion of "public" government is redundant. What else can government be but public? In the Canadian context, however, Indigenous self-government is increasingly emerging as an alternative. Public government simply means that residents are eligible to receive government programmes and services regardless of their cultural or ethnic background, and all residents are entitled to vote and run for public office (subject to the usual age and length-of-residence provisions). No consistent definition of Indigenous self-government is possible; significant variations in principle and real-life operation are legion. At its heart, however, is an element of exclusivity: to some degree most government services and political rights are restricted to Indigenous people (Alcantara and Whitfield 2010).

This chapter compares the governance structures and practices of the Nunatsiavut Government and the Government of Nunavut, not with the objective of determining whether public or self-government is better but rather to highlight similarities and differences and their implications for political representation, inclusiveness, and participation. It is not for us to declare one approach "better." Instead, we hope our comparison will help Inuit better understand the effects of their institutional design choices and whether reforms are needed to achieve the priorities of their residents, beneficiaries, and political leaders.

The chapter begins by sketching out an analytic framework for analyzing the governance regimes in Nunatsiavut and Nunavut, with particular emphasis on two essential democratic principles that have been identified in the regions as being important: representation (which entails inclusiveness) and participation. It then sets out the context within which each government operates—the purpose and the nature of the two land claims, the sociodemographic characteristics of Nunatsiavut and Nunavut, and key features of the two jurisdictions such as Nunavut's status as a stand-alone territory in contrast to Nunatsiavut's nesting within a province. We then look at government structures and operations in terms of the two governance principles and provide some observations about self-government and public government in Nunatsiavut and Nunavut.

ANALYTICAL FRAMEWORK

Scholars writing about Indigenous governance have tended to adopt a broad perspective, focusing on the normative and colonial underpinnings of the various governance models that currently exist in Canada and assessing them against alternative models that have yet to emerge, such as nation to nation and certain forms of third order of government. Some writers have focused on describing individual cases of Indigenous governance, teasing out their implications for decolonization and the pursuit of Indigenous self-determination. A strong current throughout much of this work is the debate over whether Indigenous self-government as currently practiced in Canada can actually generate meaningful self-determination, autonomy, and justice for Indigenous communities (Alfred 2005; Flanagan 2008; Irlbacher-Fox 2010).

In this chapter, we contribute to the literature in two ways. First, rather than focusing on a single case study or the broad architecture of Indigenous governance policy, we offer a comparative analysis of institutions and processes of two Inuit governance regimes. Second, we analyze the governance structures in Nunavut and Nunatsiavut by focusing on two criteria that have been identified by both communities as crucial to their functioning and existence: representation and participation. These principles are hardly unique to Inuit governance regimes; they are also at the heart of Canadian democracy.

In employing these terms, we draw upon the Canadian Democratic Audit series, published by UBC Press in the 2000s. Written by some of Canada's leading political scientists, these books analyzed and assessed a variety of Canadian political institutions against three benchmarks: inclusiveness, responsiveness, and participation (Cross 2010). In this chapter we reframe and incorporate the principle of inclusiveness into the concept of representation and exclude responsiveness due to lack of space.

An important element of representation is the extent to which those who serve in political/governmental institutions such as legislatures, executives, and bureaucracies are demographically representative of the general population. This notion of descriptive representation, sometimes called mirror or numeric representation (Lawless 2004; Mansbridge 1999), refers to a representative's characteristics and focuses on "being something rather than doing something" (Pitkin 1967, 61). This perspective holds that by virtue of a correspondence of characteristics or a "resemblance or reflection" (61) representatives are "typical of the larger class of persons they represent" (Mansbridge 1999, 629).

Assessing representation also entails analysis of other structural and operational features of governance through which peoples' ideas and preferences are brought forward to decision makers. Thus, in contrast to descriptive representation, substantive representation is more of an "acting on behalf of" mode of representation. Hanna F. Pitkin argues that an overemphasis on descriptive forms of representation ignores more salient concerns regarding how representatives actually

behave (1967, 226). A legislature may be diverse but may not produce policies that correspond to its constituents' expectations or
wishes. Instead, Pitkin emphasizes the importance of the legislative
activities of representatives and the ways in which they "act in the
interest of the represented, and in a manner responsive to them" (5).
A representative must be responsive to the "wishes, needs, and interests" (114) of the represented and must pursue these perspectives in
the political domain. That is, the actions and opinions of a representative ought to closely correspond with those of the constituency for
which he or she acts.

Inclusiveness refers to the extent to which "institutions and organizations try to ensure that certain segments of society are not excluded from becoming a member of the group" (Docherty 2005, 8).
An especially notable illustration is found in the increasing concern
of governments, Inuit and non-Inuit, about the participation of
women in political processes.

The Canadian Democratic Audit authors define participation as
the "opportunities [that] are available for members to undertake
their responsibilities" (Docherty 2005, 10). Key indicators of participation are the rates at which potential voters actually turn out to cast
their ballots at election time and the number and range of persons
who put themselves forward as candidates. However, these are by no
means the only channels of participation. For example, a participatory
governance regime provides opportunities for members of the political community to make their views known directly to decision makers on important policy issues.

The extent to which a governmental institution is representative
and inclusive and fosters participation is affected by a host of formal and informal rules, incentives, and barriers. A constitution, for
instance, may stipulate that political and legal institutions provide

citizens with multiple opportunities for formal participation in government decision making. However, it may be that informal requirements, such as time, financial resources, and expertise, prevent members of certain demographic groups from being able to actually participate. In Canada, although all adult citizens are legally entitled to run for office in national, provincial/territorial, and municipal elections, in practice a number of informal barriers related to money, class, and gender restrict the range of persons who can put their names forward for consideration in elections (Docherty 2005, 31–44).

The two benchmarks of representation and participation form the core conceptual anchors of our analysis of the governance structures in Nunatsiavut and Nunavut. We focus on these concepts because the Inuit communities of Nunatsiavut and Nunavut have made it clear that these are important objectives for their governments. In Nunatsiavut, twenty-four out of twenty-five founding principles in the Labrador Inuit Constitution address the role of Labrador Inuit in the political, cultural, economic, and social systems of Nunatsiavut. Only one subsection explicitly deals with the role and place of non-Inuit in the region: section 1.1.3 (w) states that the Labrador Inuit recognize "that people other than Labrador Inuit live in Nunatsiavut, that Nunatsiavut is part of the Canadian federation and that, therefore, Labrador Inuit political, social, cultural and economic institutions must develop policies that *embrace pluralism* within Nunatsiavut and in dealing with other peoples and their governments" (emphasis added).

The Labrador Inuit Constitution also speaks to who may participate in the political community and through what means. A number of provisions address Labrador Inuit personal autonomy, calling on Inuit to take care of themselves, their families, and the wider Inuit community (Nunatsiavut 2005, ss. 1.1.3 [f], [g], and [l]).

Other provisions recognize the range of individual legal and political rights that Inuit have in the region; these include gender rights, language rights, resource and land rights, and all of the rights and freedoms found in the *Canadian Charter of Rights and Freedoms* (ss. 1.1.3 [h–j]). The founding provisions also emphasize that Inuit political participation is to occur through democratic processes, institutions, and means (s. 1.1.3 [m]).

Nunavut—like most Canadian provinces and territories—lacks a formal constitutional document. However, shortly after their election in 1999, members of the First Nunavut Assembly developed a set of foundational precepts to guide their work and that of their successors. *Pinasuaqtavut: That Which We Have Set Out to Do: Our Hopes and Plans for Nunavut (The Bathurst Mandate)* consists of several dozen principles and guidelines that serve not as enforceable constitutional requirements, framed in terms of rights, but as strongly held convictions about Nunavut's raison d'être. *The Bathurst Mandate* includes the following:

- The health of Nunavut depends on the health of each of its physical, social, economic and cultural communities, and the ability of those communities to serve Nunavummiut [the people of Nunavut] in the spirit of *Inuuqatigiittiarniq*; the healthy inter-connection of mind, body, spirit and environment.

- Simplicity in the processes of government encourages access by all; makes the tasks more focused and more achievable; and invites participation.

- *Inuit Qaujimajatuqangit* will provide the context in which we develop an open, responsive and accountable government.

- By developing programs and services which are fair, under-

standable and easy to access we will encourage public participation and create accountability.

Among the commitments and goals *The Bathurst Mandate* held
out for the Nunavut of 2020 were the following:

- Well informed individuals and communities have the capacity and exercise responsibility for decision making;
- The Government of Nunavut conducts its business with
  openness and honesty, encouraging public input;
- We have a representative workforce in all sectors.

In short, the founding documents indicate that the Inuit in
Nunavut and Nunatsiavut believe in the classic democratic values of
representation, inclusiveness, and participation.

CONTEXT

Nunatsiavut and Nunavut share many fundamentally important features—in culture, demographics, socio-economic characteristics,
and so on—but in order to compare governance regimes, attention
to differences as well as to similarities is needed.

The Claims

Comprehensive land claims, which the Government of Canada recognizes as modern treaties, entail an exchange by which an Indigenous group formally conveys legal title to its traditional lands to the
Crown in return for a range of payments, fee simple ownership of
substantial parcels of land and other benefits. Comprehensive claims
also involve governance provisions, which vary widely, even among

the Inuit claims (Alcantara 2013). In this respect, the Nunatsiavut and Nunavut claims diverge substantially.

The Nunavut Land Claims Agreement (NLCA) was finalized in 1993 after nearly two decades of negotiations. Many important features of the claim, such as the system of co-management boards, were in place as of 1993 or shortly after, though, given the magnitude of the task of creating a territorial-level government essentially from scratch, the territory and government of Nunavut did not come into being until 1999. Although creating Nunavut as a stand-alone jurisdiction was a long-held Inuit aspiration, it was almost literally at the last moment that federal negotiators agreed to the inclusion in the claim of a provision to establish a separate territory of Nunavut (Hicks and White 2015, 46). Accordingly, the Inuit leadership had devoted little time or energy to thinking through the nature of a Nunavut government. Moreover, though in the end the federal government was willing to accept a new territory with a public government, it was clear that Canada would not agree to a stand-alone "ethnic" (i.e., Inuit self-government) territorial government, given the country's continuing existential crisis of Quebec separatism. Only after the Nunavut claim was settled did the federal government change its explicit policy of refusing to discuss self-government in land claims negotiations, thus opening the door for the self-government provisions of the Nunatsiavut claim, among others.

Like all modern treaties, the Nunavut land claim contains a wide range of features designed to preserve and enhance Inuit culture while improving social and economic conditions and ensuring extensive Inuit influence on wildlife management and environmental regulation. However, it says almost nothing about the creation and nature of the Government of Nunavut, leaving that task to a federal statute, the Nunavut Act, passed in 1993.

The Labrador Inuit Land Claims Agreement, which came into effect in 2005, was the result of twenty-eight years of on-and-off negotiations with the federal government and the Government of Newfoundland and Labrador. In 1977, the Labrador Inuit Association (LIA), the organization tasked with representing the interests of Labrador Inuit, submitted its land claim proposal to the federal government for consideration. Active negotiations, however, did not begin until 1985. Negotiations with the Labrador Inuit unfolded slowly for the first ten years but sped up significantly after the discovery of nickel in Voisey's Bay in the mid-1990s. The parties signed an agreement in principle in 1999 and a final agreement in 2005 (Alcantara 2013, 41–49).

In many ways, the Labrador Inuit Land Claims Agreement is similar to other modern treaties in Canada. It requires the federal and provincial governments to provide implementation funding to the Labrador Inuit and to recognize Inuit ownership and/or jurisdiction over 72,520 square kilometres of land in northern Labrador. Labrador Inuit property rights under the treaty include varying degrees of control and jurisdiction over water and water usage, ocean management, economic development, national parks, land-use planning, resource revenue sharing, environmental assessment, the harvesting of wildlife, plants, and fish, archaeological rights, and taxation. Unlike the Nunavut claim, the treaty contains extensive governance provisions, most notably a chapter on Inuit self-government, empowering the Labrador Inuit to draft and ratify a constitution, create community and regional governments, and have these governments exercise a range of province-like powers across Nunatsiavut (Alcantara 2013, 49–50).

Society and Economy

By Canadian, let alone international, standards, the populations of Nunatsiavut and Nunavut are very small, yet the number of people living in Nunatsiavut is only a fraction of that of Nunavut. As of March 2016, the population of Nunavut was 37,996, roughly 85 per cent of whom were Inuit (Statistics Canada 2017b); as of 2015 nearly 30,000 Inuit were registered as land claim beneficiaries, some of whom lived outside Nunavut (NTI 2016a, 62). The population of the Nunatsiavut Settlement Area in 2011 was 2,617, of whom 2,335 (90 per cent) were Inuit (Li and Smith 2016, 3), but this figure is misleading in that, as of 2016, some 2,265 beneficiaries of the claim lived in communities such as North West River, Sheshatshiu, Mud Lake, and Happy Valley-Goose Bay, located close to but outside of the settlement area. Another 2,383 beneficiaries lived elsewhere in Canada.[1] Nunavummiut, the people of Nunavut, live in twenty-five communities in a territory the size of western Europe extending across three

Table 1. Selected Social Data for Inuit in Nunatsiavut and Nunavut.

	Nunatsiavut	Nunavut
Percentage under 24	44	57
Median age	28.7	21.2
Percentage of crowded homes	16	39
Percentage of homes in need of major repair	31	35
Percentage speaking Inuktitut	25	89
Percentage with Inuktitut as mother tongue	25	80
Percentage of those 18–64 with post-secondary degree or diploma	33	29
Employment rate (percentage)	49.4	53.9
Percentage reporting excellent or very good health	52	42

time zones. By contrast, the Nunatsiavut Settlement Area consists of only five communities and 72,520 square kilometres.

Despite these substantial population and geographic differences, the regions share a number of social and economic characteristics. Table 1 presents data on selected social indicators for Inuit living in Nunatsiavut and Nunavut taken from the 2011 National Household Survey, the 2012 Aboriginal Peoples Survey, and the 2016 Census. Compared with all Canadians, Inuit in both jurisdictions are younger, more likely to live in crowded homes or homes in need of major repair, and have lower levels of educational achievement. At the same time, notable differences are evident, such as the remarkably low median age of Nunavummiut, the substantially higher rate of crowded housing in Nunavut and, most strikingly, the higher percentage of Inuit in Nunavut who say they are able to converse in Inuktitut—89 per cent, as compared with 21 per cent in Nunatsiavut.

Constitutional Framework

The Nunavut claim is all but silent on governance beyond establishing co-management boards that regulate wildlife and the environment. The Nunavut Act effectively serves as the territory's constitution, though rarely is it described as such. The act closely resembles those underpinning governance arrangements in Yukon and the Northwest Territories, not least in leaving unstated important principles such as the "confidence convention," which determines how governments gain and retain power. The act does specify certain essential structural and operational elements of the Nunavut government but is far from complete; for example, it says nothing about local governments.

By contrast, the Inuit self-government regime in Nunatsiavut is based in explicit foundational documents offering extensive detail on principles, structures, and operation of government. The claim includes a long chapter establishing the Labrador Inuit self-government and its institutions and enumerating their powers; other chapters specify the activities and responsibilities of various components of the Nunatsiavut Government.

The claim's self-government chapter required the Labrador Inuit to establish a formal constitution. In comparison with the oftentimes ambiguous, less than illuminating documents that serve as provincial and territorial constitutions, the Nunatsiavut constitution sets out fundamental principles of governance and extensive detail as to the structure and operation of government. The constitution begins by noting that "the Labrador Inuit Constitution Reflects the Will of the Inuit" (Nunatsiavut 2005, s. 1.1.2). Three pages of political, cultural, and ethical principles follow. The document then proceeds at length to establish structures, rules, and operational procedures for the Nunatsiavut Government. In addition to provisions discussed below relating to representation and participation, it incorporates such noteworthy and unusual features as an Inuit Charter of Rights and Responsibilities (chapter 2), which includes, among other things, a list of children's rights and declarations that every Labrador Inuk has "the right to bodily and psychological integrity which includes the right ... to make personal decisions concerning reproduction" (s. 2.4.7) and "the right to an environment that is not harmful to his or her health or well being and to have the environment protected for the benefit of present and future generations" (s. 2.4.20).

Territorial vs. Regional Status

Nunatsiavut is a region within a province. In some ways, this arrangement is constraining. Nunatsiavut depends on the Government of Newfoundland and Labrador for important services such as housing, education, and infrastructure and for significant funding.

Although Nunatsiavut's constitutionally protected claim affords it a special status within the province, the hard reality is that its residents represent less than 1 per cent of the provincial population. Conversely, being nested within a province does carry potential advantages, for example, the ability to delay drawing down jurisdictional powers until the Nunatsiavut Government is ready to take them on because the province will continue to deliver services. Similarly, the province may prove a useful ally in Nunatsiavut's financial dealings with Ottawa.

Nunavut's status as a territory means that it does not have to deal with an intermediate level of government and exercises almost all "province-like" powers. Moreover, its premier and ministers routinely participate directly in federal-provincial-territorial conferences and meetings—albeit as junior partners—that carry enormous governance and policy implications.

On the one hand, the Government of Nunavut's territorial status gives it an important edge over the Nunatsiavut Government in advancing the interests of Inuit. On the other hand, as a public government charged with responsibility for non-Inuit as well as Inuit, the Government of Nunavut cannot be as focused as the Nunatsiavut Government on representing Inuit interests. In one sense, the Government of Nunavut's advantage as a stand-alone territory is not attributable to inherent differences between public and Indigenous self-government. Viewed in another way, however, the linkage is clear: Nunavut would not have been given territorial status had it been constituted as an Inuit self-government, whereas the federal government was willing to accede to the demands of the Labrador Inuit for self-government in part because Nunatsiavut would be a regional government within a province.

INUIT REPRESENTATION IN NUNATSIAVUT AND NUNAVUT

Representation of Inuit, their interests, culture, and lifestyle is a principal objective of the Nunatsiavut Government, realized primarily through the many self-government features of the claim and the constitution. Beyond the numerous, if abstract and aspirational, principles enumerated in the constitution about Inuit culture and rights, perhaps the most notable illustration is that holding office in the Nunatsiavut Assembly is restricted to Inuit beneficiaries as is voting in assembly elections. In Nunavut, Inuit representation is bifurcated. All adult residents are entitled to vote and to run as candidates for the legislature, though the sheer weight of numbers means that Inuit dominate the territorial government. In addition, Inuit are represented by Inuit-only organizations such as NTI and the three regional Inuit associations.

Indigenous self-government and public government differ fundamentally in terms of political rights and eligibility for government services. Accordingly, it is important to examine the rules governing who can enrol as beneficiaries, who can participate in government, and who is entitled to government services in the two jurisdictions.

Beneficiary Status

In Nunatsiavut, chapter 3 of the claim sets out the rules for eligibility and enrolment as a beneficiary. In essence, an individual must satisfy three main criteria for enrolment. First, an applicant must either be an *Inuk*, a *Kablunângajuk*, or have at least *25 per cent Inuit ancestry*. An Inuk is defined as a member "of the aboriginal people of Labrador, sometimes known as Eskimos, that has traditionally used and occupied and currently uses and occupies the lands, waters and sea ice of the Labrador Inuit Land Claims Area, or any Region." A *Kablunângajuk* is defined as "an individual who is given that designation according to Inuit customs and traditions and who has: (a) Inuit ancestry; (b) no Inuit ancestry but who settled permanently in the Labrador Inuit Land Claims Area before 1940; or (c) no Inuit ancestry but: (i) is a lineal descendant of an individual referred to in clause (b); and (ii) was born on or before November 30th, 1990" (Canada 2004, 3.1.1). The individual must be a Canadian citizen or permanent resident of Canada who is permanently resident in or connected to the Labrador Inuit Settlement Area. Individuals can demonstrate "connection" to the Labrador Inuit Settlement Area by providing evidence that they were born in the Land Claims Area, that one of their parents was born in the Land Claims Area, or that two of their grandparents were born in the Land Claims Area and are permanent residents or were at the time of their deaths (3.1.2).

The constitution assigns the beneficiary enrolment process to four regional enrolment committees composed of Inuit or Kablunân-gajuit (the plural of Kablunângajuk). The Nunatsiavut Government provides administrative support to the committees and appoints their members but has no role in specific membership decisions. Persons who are denied enrolment by an enrolment committee may apply to an Inuit Membership Appeal Board.

With beneficiary status in Nunatsiavut comes various privileges, political rights, and access to government programmes and services not available to non-beneficiaries. Under the claim, certain harvesting rights of fish, birds, wildlife, and plants are restricted to Labrador Inuit. Similarly, the Nunatsiavut Government offers educational and training support to beneficiaries through its Post-Secondary Student Support Program (PSSSP) and Inuit Pathways. The Nunatsiavut Government also offers a non-insured health benefits programme to help beneficiaries with medical, dental, and pharmacy costs not covered by federal and provincial health plans.

Criteria for gaining beneficiary status are far simpler in Nunavut. The enrolment section of the claim sets out the basic principle: "Inuit are best able to define who is an Inuk" under the claim. No blood quantum, ancestry test, or cut-off dates come into play. To be enrolled as a beneficiary one must be a Canadian citizen, "an Inuk as determined by Inuit customs and usages," who "identifies himself or herself as an Inuk" and is connected to a Nunavut community or the Nunavut Settlement Area. The process is administered by NTI. Each community has an enrolment committee that meets regularly. As in Nunatsiavut, an Enrollment Appeals Committee hears appeals from those whose applications for enrolment are denied.

Beneficiaries of the Nunavut claim have extensive, but not unlimited, hunting, gathering, and fishing rights throughout the territory not available to non-Inuit. Once enrolled, beneficiaries automatically gain membership in NTI and in the three regional Inuit associations. Only beneficiaries may be members of Hunters and Trappers Organizations, the community-based institutions that play an important role in regulating wildlife harvesting. Since Nunavut has a public government, most government services are delivered to Inuit and non-Inuit alike.

Beneficiaries are entitled to run and vote in NTI elections and elections for other Inuit associations. They are eligible for a modest range of services provided by NTI such as scholarships, bereavement and compassionate travel assistance, an Elders benefit plan (which provides limited financial assistance to Inuit Elders), and a Harvester Support Program. As well, beneficiaries share in the financial and other provisions of Inuit Impact and Benefit Agreements negotiated with mining companies and other organizations.

Political Rights

The Inuit self-government regime in Nunatsiavut has extensive exclusionary provisions: only beneficiaries are eligible to vote for members of the assembly and only Inuit may run for the presidency or for membership in assembly, meaning that the executive council—the cabinet—is entirely Inuit. Only beneficiaries are eligible to serve as AngajukKât (mayors) or as chairs of Inuit community corporations, all of whom also sit as members of the assembly though they are not eligible to become ministers.

Non-beneficiaries, who are classified by the claim as either "residents" or "new residents," have guaranteed representation at the community government level. On each community council at least one seat is reserved for new residents; the number of reserved seats is determined by the proportion of new residents in the community though it cannot exceed a quarter of council seats. Only non-beneficiaries vote for candidates for the reserved seats and they are entitled to vote for the AngajukKât.

All adult Canadian citizens of Nunavut are entitled to run and vote in assembly and local government elections. Given the numerical preponderance of Inuit in Nunavut, it is hardly surprising that the overwhelming majority of MLAs have been Inuit, though typically three or four non-Inuit win seats in each election (out of nineteen, or more recently, twenty-two seats) and almost all territorial cabinets have had at least one non-Inuit minister (often holding the powerful finance portfolio). At the municipal level, the proportion of Inuit mayors and councillors is even higher.

Both Nunatsiavut and Nunavut give beneficiaries preference in government hiring with the objective of reaching a representative level of Inuit in the public service. Section 6.2.1 (i) of the Labrador Inuit Constitution states, "the Nunatsiavut Civil Service must be broadly representative of the *Labrador Inuit* with employment and personnel management practices based on ability, objectivity, fairness and the need to achieve *broad representation of the Labrador Inuit population* in the Nunatsiavut Civil Service" (emphasis added). Article 23 of the Nunavut claim requires—without setting a deadline—that Inuit hold a "representative" number of public service positions at all levels and in all staff categories in government. Nunatsiavut seems to have been far more successful in rendering its bureaucracy Inuit. According to the government website, beneficiaries comprise nearly 90 per cent of the public services (Nunatsiavut 2016); by contrast, Nunavut has struggled to maintain a level of 50 per cent Inuit hire (Nunavut Department of Finance 2018). Under both claims the federal government is required to take measures to reach representative levels of Inuit staff in local offices; Labrador Inuit also receive priority in hiring for certain provincial government positions in the settlement area.

The preference for Labrador Inuit is also present in Nunatsiavut's judicial system, which has not yet been created despite provisions in the Labrador Inuit Constitution that allow for this to eventually occur. Section 9.2.15 of the constitution states that only an "appropriately qualified Labrador Inuk who is a fit and proper person may be appointed as a judge of the Inuit Court." Membership on the Nunatsiavut Judicial Council is more expansive and includes several non-Inuit. The council members advise the president on judicial appointments and other matters, "investigate complaints against a judge of the Inuit Court," write and revise judicial codes of conduct and make recommendations regarding financial compensation for Inuit judges, among other things (Nunatsiavut 2005, s. 9.3.6). Preference for beneficiaries is not a factor in judicial appointments in Nunavut.

Distinctive Provisions for Representation in Nunatsiavut

In addition to the political rights granted Labrador Inuit that are not enjoyed by non-Inuit, several other features of governance in Nunatsiavut speak to issues of Inuit representation. Only some are inherent to the self-government nature of the Nunatsiavut Government—though it could be argued that self-government's tolerance of, indeed preference for, innovative and unconventional practices is significant here.

First and foremost, as noted above, most Labrador Inuit live outside the Nunatsiavut Settlement Area. Other self-government regimes, for example those in Yukon, accord their citizens entitlement to government services along with the right to vote, but Nunatsiavut is distinctive, if not unique, in providing legislative seats for beneficiaries who do not live in the settlement areas established in the claims and/or self-government agreements. The chairs of the two Inuit community corporations, Sivunivut and NunaKatiget, are members of the assembly, representing Inuit who live in communities in Labrador outside the settlement area. The chairs, who must be Inuit, are ineligible to hold cabinet positions. The constitution contemplates additional community corporations.

Making provision for Inuit living just outside the settlement area is noteworthy but what is truly remarkable are the seats (two at present [2020]) for representatives of Labrador Inuit living elsewhere in Canada. These members may hold cabinet posts.

Yet another distinctive—and unique in Canada—structural feature of the Nunatsiavut Government designed to enhance representation is the inclusion as members of the assembly of the five AngajukKât. Although they are not eligible for appointment to the cabinet, they likely bring a different perspective to assembly deliberations given their involvement in local government. Giving Angajuk-Kât seats in the assembly has important implications not simply for representation but also for intergovernmental (central-community) relations as well.

The Nunavut Implementation Commission, the body charged with the design of the Nunavut government, proposed an imaginative "gender equal" structure for the Nunavut legislature but it failed to win popular approval in a plebiscite (Hicks and White 2015, 223–25). Notwithstanding that Eva Aariak served a term as premier, women's representation in the Nunavut legislature has been dismal (in the 2008 election which brought Aariak to power, she was the only woman elected in the nineteen-member House) (White 2013). In Nunatsiavut, special provisions—again, unique in Canada, if not more broadly—aim to enhance women's representation in governance processes. Section 4.14 of the Nunatsiavut constitution requires that appointment of members to assembly committees must consider "the balance of men and women." If women are underrepresented in the assembly, provision must be made in the Standing Orders (the rules of the assembly) to appoint women who are not members of the assembly to committees (in yet another unusual provision, the constitution authorizes persons who are not assembly members to serve on legislative committees).

Even more extraordinary is section 33 of the Elections Act, which requires the president to take "reasonable steps" to appoint women as candidates in constituencies in which no women have come forward to run at the close of nominations. The president has, in several instances, appointed women candidates, though none have won seats.

NTI

One of the fundamental differences between Nunatsiavut and Nunavut affecting the representation of Inuit directly reflects the nature of Inuit self-government as contrasted with Inuit-dominated public government. In 2005, when the Nunatsiavut Government came into being, the LIA disbanded and was replaced by a government in the fullest sense of the word, with many of the key people in the LIA taking on important roles in the Nunatsiavut Government. In Nunavut, NTI (the successor to the Tungavik Federation of Nunavut, which negotiated the claim) is the Inuit-only organization that, among other things, represents Inuit interests in issues of claim implementation; it continues to exist, and indeed plays a singularly powerful role in Nunavut governance.

A large, well-resourced organization dedicated to promoting Inuit interests, together with the Inuit-dominated public government, doubtless makes for an especially strong Inuit presence in Nunavut governance. NTI is certainly an effective advocate for Inuit and their interests within and beyond the territory's borders. However, it is hard to avoid the conclusion that, as an Inuit self-government whose constitutional mandate is almost entirely focused on governing on behalf of Inuit, the Nunatsiavut Government is better able to serve the interests of Inuit than is the NTI-Nunavut government combination. As a public government, the Government of Nunavut is concerned with representing all Nunavummiut, Inuit and non-Inuit, but other factors come into play as well. To be sure, NTI and the Government of Nunavut often work closely together, especially in dealings with Ottawa, and generally agree on policy direction. Still, the fact that a formal protocol—*Katujjiqatigiinniq*—sets out principles and mechanisms for their co-operation underlines the reality that these are two separate institutions with occasionally quite different perspectives and priorities. Any time two organizations operate within the same sphere the possibility of conflict arises and NTI has not hesitated to voice hard-hitting criticism of the Government of Nunavut and its policies on a range of issues, most notably perhaps on educational matters (Alcantara and Wilson 2014). Although offering Inuit different perspectives on important issues can be valuable, the conflict and bifurcation of political activity inherent in the existence of two entities can adversely affect the promotion of Inuit interests. Another concern is that at both the political and administrative levels, NTI and the Government of Nunavut are in constant competition for good people within the relatively limited talent pool available in Nunavut (Hicks and White 2015).

PARTICIPATION IN NUNAVUT AND NUNATSIAVUT

Turnout in Nunatsiavut elections varies a good deal. In the 2014 Ordinary Members election overall turnout was 46.7 per cent, but this figure obscures the wide difference in turnout between the five communities within the settlement area (68.4 per cent, with little cross-community variation—61.4 per cent to 70.6 per cent) and the Upper Lake Melville constituency (47.4 per cent) and the Canada constituency (25.8 per cent).[2] The 2018 Ordinary Members election saw a substantially different pattern of turnout: overall 39.8 per cent, with the Upper Lake Melville and Canada constituencies registering rates of 35.4 and 35.9 per cent and a turnout of 49.5 per cent in the settlement area communities. The decline in settlement area turnout reflected a drop of nearly 12 percentage points in Hopedale and a remarkable change in Nain's turnout rate: 70.6 per cent in 2014, 33.7 per cent in 2018 (turnout increased marginally in Postville and Rigolet).[3] The competitive presidential election in 2012 featured two rounds of voting, with the second round a run-off vote. In the first round, 2,132 votes were cast versus 2,183 in the second round, which translates into turnout results of 29.8 per cent and 30.5 per cent based on the number of beneficiaries—7,162—as of September 2016 (given the gap in data points, actual rates would be marginally higher). We do not have data for community government elections. Turnout in Nunatsiavut also varies substantially in federal and provincial elections. In two recent federal elections, turnout in Nunatsiavut was 62.4 per cent (2015) and 51.8 per cent (2011); in two recent provincial elections it was 38.0 per cent (2015) and 72.7 per cent (2011).[4]

Clearly, not all beneficiaries are exercising their right to vote. Although we have no systematic data to explain turnout levels or the volatility in turnout, reports from the Nunatsiavut electoral officer point to possible informational and logistical barriers to voting. One potential barrier is that voters lack sufficient information about the candidates. In her report on the 2016 presidential election, the electoral officer remarked: "I did receive a complaint that there was not enough publicity about the Presidential election. Maybe now is the time to look at better ways to get this information out to the electors" (Nunatsiavut Electoral Officer 2016, 2). Similar concerns were heard during the 2012 presidential election, according to the electoral officer: "Soon after the mail in ballots went out each day we were continually getting calls from members of the Canadian Constituency asking 'Who are these Candidates? Where can I find some information on them?'" (Nunatsiavut Electoral Officer 2012, 4). It may also be that polling stations, advance polling procedures, and mail-in ballots are inconvenient for some beneficiaries. According to the Nunatsiavut Electoral Officer in 2010, "How come I can't vote by using my computer by phone or can I fax you my ballot? is a question that was very common for our electors to ask during this election" (5). It is also worth bearing in mind that the voting age in Nunatsiavut is sixteen (versus eighteen in Nunavut and sixteen for NTI) and it is common across a wide range of political systems for turnout rates among young people to be low (Esser and de Vreese 2008).

Another indicator of participation is interest in running for elected office. Again we lack systematic data at the community government level, but a healthy number of candidates have come forward in the four elections for Ordinary Members. In the four elections (2006, 2010, 2014, and 2018) the number of candidates has ranged between twenty-two and thirty-one for the ten seats. The May 2018 election was the first in which a candidate was acclaimed—First Minister Kate Mitchell in Makkovik—and also featured the lowest number of candidates. Only time will tell whether these were temporary blips or mark the start of significant trends.

Participation rates in Nunavut-wide elections have been, with one notable exception, somewhat higher and less volatile than in Nunatsiavut, although results from the most recent territorial election may indicate that the difference is lessening. Territorial turnout has ranged from 88.6 per cent in 1999 (the first Nunavut election) to 63.3 per cent in 2017 (Rogers 2017; White 2016, Table 11.1; see also Henderson 2007, chapter 7). A few popular candidates have won by acclamation, but, overall, candidates have not been in short supply: in the four Nunavut elections 340 candidates have contested 101 seats. As in Nunatsiavut, the absence of parties, which eliminates the need to secure a party nomination, and the small numbers of voters in each constituency have meant that there are few organizational or financial barriers to candidates wishing to contest assembly elections. In federal elections, turnout in Nunavut was 45.7 per cent in 2011 and 59.4 in 2015.[5]

A striking departure from the generally healthy participation levels in Nunavut is the typically dismal turnout in NTI elections. In recent territory-wide NTI elections, barely a third or fewer beneficiaries voted (32 per cent in the 2016 presidential election, 35 per cent in the 2012 presidential election, 31 per cent in the 2014 vice-presidential election, and 32.1 per cent in the 2016 presidential election [NTI 2012, 2014, 2016b]). Low turnout contrasts with the healthy number of candidates who come forward to contest NTI elections: four and six in the 2016 and 2012 presidential elections, three for the 2014 vice-presidential race, and four in the 2016 presidential election. NTI elections at the regional level are also contested by numerous candidates yet are characterized by low turnout.

Especially in governance regimes committed to following Inuit cultural precepts, participation entails much more than voting and running for office. Both Nunavut and Nunatsiavut employ formal and informal means for encouraging public involvement in government decision making. Nunatsiavut seems to have more—and more innovative—mechanisms for promoting Inuit participation in governmental processes than does Nunavut, though further research is needed into just how effective they are. Nunatsiavut's substantially smaller scale is likely an advantage in promoting public participation.

One of the foundational principles set out in the Nunatsiavut constitution is "the belief that decision making by Labrador Inuit political, social, cultural and economic institutions should promote participation by Labrador Individuals and organizations" (Nunatsiavut 2005, s. 1.1.3 [q]). A more direct constitutionally mandated obligation speaks to women's participation:

> Recognizing that Labrador Inuit women have historically been under-represented in many of the political, social, cultural and economic institutions of Labrador Inuit society, the Nunatsiavut Assembly and the Nunatsiavut Government, the Inuit Community Governments and the Inuit Community Corporations must take practical and positive measures, which may include enactment of Inuit laws by the

Nunatsiavut Assembly, to facilitate and promote the equal
participation of Labrador Inuit women in the political social, cultural and economic institutions of Labrador Inuit
society. (Nunatsiavut 2005, s. 4.17.2)

A number of mechanisms are in place to realize these principles.
Assembly committees hold public hearings on policy and legislation.
The cabinet is required by the constitution to meet in communities outside the capital. A basic design feature of the Nunatsiavut Government,
imposed by the same section of the constitution, requires it to decen-
tralize its administrative offices to all communities, subject to economic
feasibility. At first glance this provision seems unrelated to enhancing
public participation, but one of its objectives is to bring government
operations closer to the people, thereby giving them greater opportunity
to be involved in governance processes. In a constitutional obligation
that surely must be unique across Canadian government bureaucracies,
the Nunatsiavut civil service must "respond to the needs of Inuit and
Inuit must be encouraged to participate in policy-making" (Nunatsiavut 2005, s. 6.2.1 [e]). Finally, the Nunatsiavut constitution gives the
general Inuit population a significant role in amending it. Passage of a
constitutional amendment requires, in addition to a resolution supported by 60 per cent of the members of the assembly, majority approval in a referendum (with 75 per cent support in the assembly no
referendum is required). Alternatively, a constitutional amendment
proposed by petition of 500 eligible voters must be put to a referendum
and will take effect if 60 per cent of those voting agree to it. (The president has discretion to reject frivolous or vexatious petitions or those
that he or she deems "unclear or incomplete"; petitions declared by the
president as incomplete or unclear may also be referred to the assembly
for "restatement and clarification" before referenda are held on them.)

In contrast, the Government of Nunavut seems to provide fewer opportunities for public participation. It does regularly consult Nunavummiut on policy issues; its most frequently employed mechanism involves committees of the assembly holding public hearings on policy initiatives and on proposed legislation. On major issues, committees travel across the territory though they cannot include all communities in their consultation tours. Bringing government "closer to the people" was also a key objective of the extensive decentralization built into the design of the Nunavut government. Other objectives—distributing stable white-collar jobs to communities across the territory and avoiding excessive population and logistical burdens on the capital—have been met, but enhanced public participation in governance processes has not occurred (Hicks and White 2013, 307–9).

CONCLUSION

What conclusions may be drawn from the Nunavut-Nunatsiavut comparison? Many stark contrasts are evident with some directly stemming from the fundamental difference between self-government and public government. Two are especially notable. First, in Nunatsiavut certain political rights are enjoyed by Inuit but not by non-beneficiaries. This contrasts with the political rights available to all Nunavummiut. Second is the need in Nunavut for an Inuit-only land claim organization, NTI, to represent Inuit interests to government (territorial as well as federal). Other substantial differences— distinctive features of the Nunatsiavut Government such as the inclusion of AngajukKât and the chairs of the Inuit community corporations as assembly members, the requirement that the president attempt to nominate women candidates if none come forward in elections, the reserved seats for representatives of beneficiaries across Canada, and the opportunity for beneficiaries to petition for constitutional change—are not attributable to self-government.

Or are they? To be sure the distinctive elements of the Nunatsiavut Government just enumerated are not inherent to self-government, understood as limiting political rights and government services to Indigenous people. However, a key principle of self-government is the ability—within broad limits—to design and operate government in ways that meet the political aspirations and traditions of Indigenous people. As such, self-government offers not simply the opportunity to go beyond the conventional but also the incentive to do so if it will meet and further the people's political goals. Public government, at least in Canada, has limited tolerance for experimentation and for distinctive design features, even if they would not compromise its "public" nature. Self-government, by contrast, as the example of Nunatsiavut confirms, is characterized by a search for the most appropriate and effective governance forms, be they orthodox or unconventional.

ACKNOWLEDGEMENTS

This paper was financially supported by the Tradition and Transition Project, which is co-sponsored by the Nunatsiavut Government and Memorial University and funded by SSHRC. We thank Jeremy Roberts for research assistance.

NOTES

1   We are grateful to the Nunatsiavut Registrar of Beneficiaries for data on the number and location of beneficiaries.
2   Figures calculated from data in OKâlaKatiget Society, 2014.
3   Figures calculated from data in Nunatsiavut Government, 2018.

4 Data sources: federal—http://www.elections.ca/res/rep/off/ovr2015app/41/9691e.html; http://www.elections.ca/scripts/ovr2011/default.html; provincial—http://www.assembly.nl.ca/business/electronicdocuments/GeneralElection2011-Report.pdf; http://www.elections.gov.nl.ca/elections/. Note that federal and provincial turnout figures reflect only voters in the five communities within the Labrador Inuit Settlement Area.

5 Data sources: http://www.elections.ca/scripts/ovr2011/default.html; http://www.elections.ca/res/rep/off/ovr2015app/41/9770e.html.

REFERENCES

Alcantara, Christopher. 2013. *Negotiating the Deal: Comprehensive Land Claims Agreements in Canada.* Toronto: University of Toronto Press.

Alcantara, Christopher, and Gary N. Wilson. 2014. "The Dynamics of Intrajurisdictional Relations in the Inuit Regions of the Canadian Arctic: An Institutionalist Perspective." *Regional and Federal Studies* 24, no. 1: 43–61.

Alcantara, Christopher, and Greg Whitfield. 2010. "Aboriginal Self-Government through Constitutional Design." *Journal of Canadian Studies* 44, no. 2: 122–45.

Alfred, Taiaike. 2005. *Wasáse: Indigenous Pathways of Action and Freedom.* Peterborough, ON: Broadview.

Arrigada, Paul. 2016. "Inuit: Fact Sheet for Nunavut." Statistics Canada Catalogue No. 89-656-X2016017.

Canada. 2004. *Land Claims Agreement between the Inuit of Labrador and Her Majesty the Queen in Right of Newfoundland and Labrador and Her Majesty the Queen in Right of Canada.* Ottawa: Minister of Public Works and Government Services.

Cross, William. 2010. "Constructing the Canadian Democratic Audit." In *Auditing Canadian Democracy*, edited by William Cross, 1–17. Vancouver: UBC Press.

Docherty, David. 2005. *Legislatures.* Vancouver: UBC Press.

Elections Newfoundland and Labrador. 2015. *Provincial General Election Report.* St. John's.

Esser, Frank, and Claes H. de Vreese. 2007. "Comparing Young Voters' Political Engagement in the United States and Europe." *American Behavioral Scientist* 50, no. 9: 1195–213.

Flanagan, Tom. 2008. *First Nations? Second Thoughts.* Montreal and Kingston: McGill-Queen's University Press.

Hicks, Jack, and Graham White. 2015. *Made in Nunavut: An Experiment in Decentralized Government.* Vancouver: UBC Press.

Irlbacher-Fox, Stephanie. 2010. *Finding Dahshaa: Self-Government, Social Suffering, and Aboriginal Policy in Canada.* Vancouver: UBC Press.

Lawless, Jennifer L. 2004. "Politics of Presence? Congresswomen and Symbolic Representation." *Political Research Quarterly* 57, no. 1: 81–99.

Li, Shirley, and Kristina Smith. 2016. "Inuit: Fact Sheet for Nunatsiavut." Statistics Canada Catalogue No. 89-656-X2016015.

Mansbridge, Jane. 1999. "Should Blacks Represent Blacks and Women Represent Women? A Contingent Yes." *The Journal of Politics* 61, no. 3: 628–57.

Nunatsiavut. 2005. *Nunatsiavut Constitution Act* (CIL 31-12-2012 N-3) ("The Labrador Inuit Constitution").

Nunatsiavut. 2016. http://www.nunatsiavut.com/department/human-resources/.

Nunatsiavut Electoral Officer. 2010. "Report to the Speaker Nunatsiavut Assembly: Ordinary Members Election May 4, 2010."

Nunatsiavut Electoral Officer. 2012. "Report to the Nunatsiavut Assembly: The Presidential Elections of May 1, 2012 and the Run Off Election of June 11, 2012."

Nunatsiavut Electoral Officer. 2016. Letter to Kate Mitchell, First Minister re 2016 Presidential Election. May 4, 2016.

Nunatsiavut Government. 2018. "Official Election Results Released." Media release, May 7, 2018. https://www.nunatsiavut.com/article/official-election-results-released/.

Nunavut Department of Finance. 2018. "Towards a Representative Public Service: Statistics of the Public Service within the Government of Nunavut as of June 30, 2018." https://www.nunatsiavut.com/article/official-election-results-released/.

Nunavut Tunngavik Incorporated (NTI). 2012. "Cathy Towtongie Re-Elected President of NTI." Media release, December 11, 2012. https://www.tunngavik.com/news/cathy-towtongie-re-elected-president-of-nti/.

Nunavut Tunngavik Incorporated (NTI). 2014. "James Eetoolook Re-elected NTI Vice-President." Media release, December 9, 2014. https://www.tunngavik.com/news/james-eetoolook-re-elected-nti-vice-president/.

Nunavut Tunngavik Incorporated (NTI). 2016a. *Annual Report 2014–15*. Iqaluit. https://www.tunngavik.com/publication_categories/nti-annual-reports/.

Nunavut Tunngavik Incorporated (NTI). 2016b. "NTI Announces Unofficial Results of Presidential Election." Media release, December 13, 2016. https://www.tunngavik.com/2016/12/13/nti-announces-unofficial-results-of-presidential/.

OKâlaKatiget Society. 2014. "NG Election Results (Unofficial)." May 6, 2014. www.okosociety.com/?p=10336.

Pitkin, Hanna F. 1967. *The Concept of Representation*. Berkeley: University of California Press.

Rogers, Sarah. 2017. "63.3 Per cent of Nunavut Voters Cast Ballots in 2017 Election." *Nunatsiaq News*. November 8, 2017. https://nunatsiaq.com/stories/article/6567463-3_per_cent_of_nunavut_voters_cast_ballots_in_2017_election/.

Statistics Canada. 2017a. "Canada's Population Estimates, Second Quarter 2017." Media release, September 27, 2017. https://www150.statcan.gc.ca/n1/daily-quotidien/170927/dq170927e-eng.htm.

Statistics Canada. 2017b. "The Aboriginal Languages of First Nations People, Métis and Inuit." Media release, October 25, 2017. https://www12.statcan.gc.ca/census-recensement/2016/as-sa/98-200-x/2016022/98-200-x2016022-eng.cfm.

White, Graham. 2005. *Cabinets and First Ministers*. Vancouver: UBC Press.

White, Graham. 2013. "In the Presence of Northern Aboriginal Women? Women in Territorial Politics." In *Stalled: The Representation of Women in Canadian Governments*, edited by Linda Trimble, Jane Arscott, and Manon Tremblay, 233–52. Vancouver: UBC Press.

White, Graham. 2016. "The Territories." In *Big Worlds: Politics and Elections in the Canadian Provinces and Territories*, edited by Jared J. Wesley, 184–205. Toronto: University of Toronto Press.

Wilson, Gary, Christopher Alcantara, and Thierry Rodon. 2020. *Nested Federalism and Inuit Governance in the Canadian Arctic*. Vancouver: UBC Press.

Reclaiming Inuit Knowledge in Pursuit of Self-Governance: Regulating Research through Relationships

Amy Hudson and Julie Bull

INTRODUCTION

This chapter demonstrates the connections between Indigenous self-governance and research governance in the context of relationships between researchers, community members, and the land. Informed by the lessons learned through community-led sustainability research in three pilot communities in the Inuit territory of Nunatu-Kavut, research experiences over time in NunatuKavut, including the 2006 research ethics review (Brunger and Bull 2011), and ongoing research governance work that seeks to further enhance and build on research ethics protocols, this chapter explains how Inuit autonomy in research is an expression of self-governance and creates pathways for Inuit self-determination. From an Inuit governance perspective, the role of Inuit-led research in communities is a tool for community and cultural preservation. Research grounded in relationships based on respect and reciprocity further enhances community capacity and outcomes by building on the strengths, expertise, and local knowledge of Inuit in their time and place.

BACKGROUND

NunatuKavut, which means "our ancient land," refers to the homeland of approximately 6,000 Inuit belonging to southeast and central Labrador in the province of Newfoundland and Labrador. Labrador's southeast coastal communities are remote, and some are fly in/out with a seasonal ferry service during summer months only. Although there is road connection to most communities along the southeast coast due to the fairly recent Trans-Labrador Highway (TLH), the road itself is gravel (with some paved sections) without cell service or other amenities. Some NunatuKavut communities face varying degrees of water and food insecurity, and one remote community (Black Tickle) has no fuel or gas provider. Yet, NunatuKavut Inuit remain committed to life in their communities and maintain a connection to the land, sea, and ice as did their ancestors.

The NunatuKavut Community Council (NCC), an Inuit rights-based governing organization, represents the Indigenous rights for NunatuKavut Inuit. The council of elected officials representing six regions throughout NunatuKavut includes a president and vice-president. Its six departments respond to the interests, priorities, and needs of NunatuKavut communities: Office of the CEO; Research, Education and Culture; Environment and Natural Resources; Employment and Skills Development; Finance and Administration; Health and Social; and the Labrador West Indigenous Service Centre.

The NCC asserts self-determination in research and governance. In this context, it has led research initiatives that respond to community priorities, needs, and interests. One initiative builds upon Inuit governance and sustainable communities through self-determined research; this research will be referenced throughout the ensuing discussion. In sum, the NunatuKavut governance and sustainability research aims to bridge the gap between governance and political theory and practice in NunatuKavut. Further, this research assists in the translation and articulation of Inuit perspectives and worldviews that will create opportunities for resurgence and self-determination, enlightened by Inuit knowledge-holders in NunatuKavut. As the NCC continues to protect and ensure the rights of Inuit in Nunatu-Kavut, community expectations of NCC's governance role in Nunatu-Kavut expands.

This chapter discusses the foundational role of relationships in regulating research in Indigenous communities generally and Inuit communities in NunatuKavut specifically. The interconnections between Inuit governance and research is supported by examples of research governance and leadership in NunatuKavut. Finally, pathways to self-determination through current community sustainability research in NunatuKavut are addressed, connecting the importance of autonomous and community-driven research to governance discussions.

POSITIONALITY OF AUTHORS

Given the importance of accountability to and in Indigenous research, as co-authors we position ourselves within this discussion. Being aware of why we do what we do and who it impacts and how is a vital consideration in our dual role as researchers belonging to Indigenous communities. As co-author, I (Hudson) have led the Nunatu-Kavut governance and sustainability research in my capacity as NCC research manager and as part of my PhD research, while I (co-author Bull) have been integral to informing NCC's founding research policy and ethics practice. In addition, we co-lead NCC's most recent research governance and ethics work that will later be discussed in further detail later in this chapter.

Amy Hudson

I was born and raised in the NunatuKavut community of Black Tickle, a remote island community on Labrador's southeast coast. As an Indigenous researcher and community member it is integral that I position my approach to the governance and sustainability research that I am engaged in. My connection to homeland, people, and my Indigenous community ground my sense of relationality and responsibility in and to my work. My regard for research as a tool for community and cultural preservation is related to my knowledge of the history of Indigenous peoples and NunatuKavut Inuit specifically as it relates to this work. As a result, Indigenous ways of knowing and being were embraced and prioritized in this research project.

Since 2014, I have been living, learning, and working among and with Inuit communities in NunatuKavut, Labrador, in diverse areas of research and have demonstrated leadership within the NCC. Throughout this time, I have been sharing, learning, relearning, and reclaiming my Inuit history, past and present, in a renewed light. I have been immersed in the idea of research as a tool for community betterment and sustainability. In many respects, my participation in research, as a community member, researcher, and knowledge-holder, among my peers and fellow community members, has informed and inspired a nuanced and intricate awareness and understanding of governance from the cultural vantage point of NunatuKavut Inuit. To share my understandings of our world and its teachings with others is both humbling and significant, as Inuit have not been immune to the narratives and falsehoods produced and reproduced by colonially rooted research practices. Further conversations with friend, colleague, and co-author Julie Bull have grounded our respective fields of work (Hudson in Indigenous governance, Bull in research ethics) as that which cannot be separated from one another.

In discussing our respective research and experiences, we became increasingly aware of the connections and interconnections between our areas of research focus. Our mutual understandings of the role of research, in Indigenous communities, along with our commitment to Indigenous resurgence and self-determination in research, found us collaborating and supporting one another in our research, building on one another's expertise, and working together to support Inuit self-determination in our homeland. I am a PhD candidate in the Interdisciplinary program, Memorial University, and lead on the aforementioned Inuit community governance and sustainability research.

Julie Bull

I am a researcher, educator, ethicist, and poet originally from Happy Valley-Goose Bay. I am Inuk from NunatuKavut, with familial and ancestral ties to the Sandwich Bay area on Labrador's southeast coast. A fierce advocate for Indigenous rights, I have been instrumental in building relationships between academic institutions, governments, and Indigenous communities throughout Canada. My collaborative research approaches have garnered international attention as I work diligently to ensure that Indigenous people are fairly treated and compensated and that research, education, and program development does not occur without community consent. While my area of focus is research methods and ethics, my approach crosses disciplines and sectors, which make me an excellent promoter of relational approaches to partnerships between Indigenous and non-Indigenous people. As the first high school graduate in my family, I am no stranger to pioneering and forging a path on the road less travelled. I am not held back by obstacles and I find solutions to problems. My commitment and dedication to advancing my education is not just for my own benefit, as I knew that this formal education was a ticket to places and possibilities that many in my community never had and a way for me to give back to the community that supported me. For the past fifteen years, I have advanced through various roles, from Project Management in Education, to Research and Policy Management for Indigenous leadership, to teaching at the university level, and I have been called around the world to speak on Indigenous issues. Long before the Truth and Reconciliation Commission Calls to Action (TRC) was launched, I advised various organizations how to build relationships with Indigenous communities and how to work toward reconciliation. I am especially keen to work with other influencers and innovators who use their positions of privilege to challenge the status quo and to build meaningful and sustainable relationships with Indigenous peoples by decolonizing the systems that continue to oppress us.

CONNECTING INDIGENOUS GOVERNANCE TO RESEARCH

Leading Indigenous scholars Jeff Corntassel and Glen Coulthard have made significant contributions to the scholarly literature relating to Indigenous rights and self-determination. Corntassel's (2008, 2012) work, in particular, provides theoretical and practical insight into how Indigenous nations can regenerate and become sustainable and self-determining nations. Coulthard (2014) questions the utility of Canada's recognition of Indigenous rights rhetoric and proposes an alternative understanding of Canada-Indigenous relations in this context, one that is critical and enlightened. These scholars point to the need for Indigenous autonomy on Indigenous homelands. The autonomy to make decisions on one's own lands and exercise good governance (in the ways described above) extend to all realms of decision making, including research.

Furthermore, numerous Indigenous scholars (Bull 2010; Kovach 2009; Smith 2012; Wilson 2008) cite the need for Indigenous autonomy and self-determination in research with and by Indigenous peoples and upon Indigenous lands. These scholars have paved the way, proposing decolonizing approaches to research that reflect Indigenous ways of knowing and being, all of which point to the important role of relationships in determining research priorities and carrying out community research. This understanding that relationships are integral to governing research is influenced by such scholars as Shawn Wilson, who explains:

> We are beginning to articulate our own research paradigms and to demand that research conducted in our communities follows our codes of conduct and honors our systems of knowledge and worldviews. Research by and for Indigenous peoples is a ceremony that brings relationships together. (2008, 8)

Understanding the interconnectedness of Indigenous and research governance requires an understanding of a colonial history of research upon Indigenous peoples and their lands. Historically, research has been conducted "on" Indigenous peoples, about Indigenous peoples, and without their consent (Bull 2016). The western approach to research and the subsequent production of knowledge from a western perspective has had, and continues to have, negative implications for Indigenous peoples and their communities and for their ability to self-determine. Research conducted from a western perspective, and as expressed by Linda Tuhiwai Smith (2012), the

resulting relationship between researcher and researched has also
served to oppress Indigenous peoples as the western researcher/
scholar/academic occupies the role of knowledge-holder and decision maker, wielding power, authority, and control over those being
"researched." This power relationship is further perpetuated within
academia and then within Indigenous communities themselves, as
Indigenous peoples continue to experience colonization by western
ways of thinking, being, seeing, and doing. Indeed, a history of research "on" Indigenous peoples has demonstrated that such research
has the power and ability to displace, shame, create barriers, inflict
harm, and create chaos on the lives of Indigenous peoples. Lester-
Irabinna Rigney states:

> The research enterprise as a vehicle for investigation has
> poked, prodded, measured, tested, and compared data to-
> ward understanding Indigenous cultures and human nature.
> Explorers, medical practitioners, intellectuals, travelers, and
> voyeurs who observed from a distance have all played a role
> in the scientific scrutiny of Indigenous peoples. (1999, 109)

This colonial research approach, which marginalizes and sup-
presses Indigenous voice and agency in the research relationship, reflects a foreign understanding of and awareness about relationships
that is not conducive to Indigenous self-determination into the future.

Smith states that "research can no longer be conducted with Indigenous communities as if their views did not count or their lives did not
matter" (2012, 10). Margaret Kovach explains that "cultural longevity
depends on the ability to sustain cultural knowledge" (2009, 12). These
Indigenous scholars point to Indigenous participation in research that
is Indigenous-led and Indigenous-centred. Inuit governments and

governing organizations such as Inuit Tapiriit Kanatami (ITK) and NCC are moving toward regaining control of decision making and regaining autonomy on their lands, through research. Both have clearly identified the need for Inuit autonomy and self-determination in research. Both NCC and ITK have cited their negative experiences when research priorities are developed and decisions are made by outside institutions and external researchers without Inuit and community consent. In 2018, ITK released a document entitled "National Inuit Strategy on Research" which highlights that Inuit must have autonomy in the research relationship, citing that "research is a tool for creating social equity" (ITK 2018, 9) and articulating a research vision:

> Inuit vision research producing new knowledge that empowers our people in meeting the needs and priorities of our families and communities. We see achieving self-determination in research as the means for ensuring that research governance bodies, policies, and practices are consistent with this vision. (7)

The significance of Indigenous peoples' ability to make decisions that impact them and their communities, in research relationships, is demonstrated as many Indigenous nations, scholars, and community members deem it necessary in the pursuit of decolonizing research and research practices (Bull 2016; Martin 2012; Smith 2012; Wilson 2008).

RESEARCH IN NUNATUKAVUT

We (Bull and Hudson) have collaborated with NCC (and others) in an effort to establish robust research ethics and governance in NunatuKavut. As conversations and actions occurred regarding NCC's governance more generally, a parallel process of advancing research governance specifically happened independently and interrelatedly (Bull and Hudson 2018). As a governing organization with a commitment to self-determination, the NCC recognizes that the ability of Inuit to self-determine in research requires that research be guided, informed, and prioritized by Inuit. NCC staff, partners, and collaborators have worked for many years to advance opportunities for community self-determination in research in NunatuKavut, thinking many generations ahead to the youth and children of the future, and leading from the future as it emerges in relation to research ethics oversight in their territory. This began with a formalized research review process in 2006 (with subsequent and substantial revisions between 2010 and 2013) (Brunger and Bull 2011; Brunger and Russell 2015; Brunger and Wall 2016; Brunger, Bull, and Wall 2014). As of 2020, NCC is updating its research ethics and engagement policies to reflect the evolution since 2013. Like many other governing bodies, NCC promotes and endorses research that is relational, beneficial, collaborative, and relevant.

While Canada's commitment to Indigenous reconciliation in research and education is important and welcomed, this new vision has not come without generations of Indigenous peoples' efforts and struggles for autonomy in research on their lands. For decades, Indigenous peoples have asserted their autonomy, challenging and resisting governments, institutions, and practices that continue to marginalize and oppress Indigenous peoples on their own lands. This is especially evident in the way in which research "about and on" NunatuKavut Inuit, including settler interpretations of historical evidence, continue to marginalize and oppress the role and voice of Inuit women in Inuit society and community in NunatuKavut. Indeed, approaches that use western biases to inform scholarly literature has often undermined Indigenous people's knowledge and expertise. According to Indigenous scholar Leanne Leddy:

> The practice of reading historical evidence without interrogating the settler biases and misunderstandings contributes to a view of Indigenous cultural systems as stagnant, unchanging, and backwards, the very historical lens that scholars, Supreme Court decisions, and most importantly, Indigenous voices have sought to change. (2018, 212)

In contrast, I (co-author Hudson) am co-leading anti-colonial and action-oriented research in Inuit (traditional) education and Inuit women's history in NunatuKavut. This research facilitates opportunities for NunatuKavut Inuit to share, re-learn, and reclaim culture and history through secondary education, while privileging community knowledge-holders as teachers of community youth. Through interviews and storytelling with Inuit women in NunatuKavut, we build upon and privilege NunatuKavut Inuit cultural knowledge and identify community priorities, from the vantage of Inuit women. This research is a direct response to colonial research practices that have marginalized and oppressed the role and agency of Inuit women from NunatuKavut society.

Research that privileged the vantage of the male explorer to Labrador while ignoring Inuit agency has also perpetuated false narratives of people and place that have had, and continues to have, detrimental implications on NunatuKavut Inuit. As a result, NunatuKavut Inuit have been omitted from an array of programming and services for Inuit (e.g., federal programs and services) and have been inaccurately represented in the scholarly literature, education, and curriculum (Moore, Hudson, and Maxwell 2018). For example, the provincial curriculum in secondary schools in Newfoundland and Labrador often marginalizes NunatuKavut Inuit history and culture or represents NunatuKavut Inuit inaccurately. Other stories told by outsiders (primarily non-Indigenous researchers, travellers, etc.) have attempted to understand and quantify the level of Inuit-ness among Inuit on the south coast of Labrador over time, without awareness or consideration of outsider bias. The consequences of research "on and about" NunatuKavut Inuit has had diverse, negative impacts on NunatuKavut Inuit and, ultimately, their ability to self-determine. Yet, the NCC, on behalf of NunatuKavut Inuit, have resisted colonial research practices, such as the above, and have reclaimed autonomy in research relationships, with increasing capacity to govern research practices and set their own research priorities (Bull and Hudson 2018).

For Inuit-governing organizations, such as the NCC, a clear link exists between research, well-being, and Inuit self-determination. In an article by Ashlee Cunsolo and Hudson about research and relationships in northern-led research, Hudson states the following about the role of self-governance in conducting research in NunatuKavut:

> Our commitment to self-determination through research, and the fundamental importance of research to our communities, exists beyond an ideal of social justice. We are committed to research for our survival. It is about reclaiming who we are and where come from and continue to belong as a people, as we continue the decolonizing work synonymous with our Indigenous resistance and cultural preservation efforts. (2018, 26)

Western research protocols that do not reflect Inuit ways of knowing and being have been imposed over time, and some of the noted impacts are described above. Through their very existence and socialization into society, these protocols continue to deny and/or erase Inuit agency in NunatuKavut through privileging outsider worldviews. Over time, these outside ideas fostered a particular knowledge base, supporting theories of acculturation and assimilation among Inuit. Examples of research and research practices, such as these that deny and invalidate Indigenous existence and claims to territory, are indicative of a time and culture that regarded Indigenous peoples as subjects to be known, studied, and saved by outsiders; this style of research is being challenged by leading Indigenous scholars such as Wilson, Kovach, and Smith, among others.

Despite a history of colonially rooted research practices upon Indigenous peoples that has rendered Indigenous knowledge inferior to that of western ways of thinking, Indigenous peoples in Canada have been engaged in and leading research since time immemorial (Stewart-Harawira 2013). Indigenous peoples have worked to inform and produce their own forms of research practices that reflect Indigenous culture, history, and values (Wilson 2008). For many Indigenous communities, and indeed for the NCC as governors of research in their territory, the ideal research relationship is one whereby research priorities are identified by the community, and any consequential research is led by the goals, values, and interests of the community itself. The NCC shares ITK's philosophy that research can be a tool for positive change and an avenue through which Inuit should, and must, exert autonomy and leadership. The NCC has committed to furthering the establishment of its research governance policies and protocols, which reflect NunatuKavut community values and principles. The NCC, as of 2020, is leading a research governance initiative in NunatuKavut. In doing so, we are working with NunatuKavut communities and NCC departments to distinguish best practices for identifying strategic research that benefits and interests communities. Further, this work will build upon existing community engagement documents and research protocols to ensure that research governance practices will meet the needs and interests of NunatuKavut Inuit. This work is indicative of the leadership role NCC has taken in research and the awareness of the role of research in community and cultural survival. The anti-colonial research described by co-author Hudson (above) exemplifies self-determining research by Inuit and demonstrates community commitment to counter colonial research practices and to seek out more beneficial research relationships that align with community priorities.

In NunatuKavut, governance and research cannot exist in isolation from each other. If we are to speak of regulating research in NunatuKavut communities, we must understand that at the core, and central to Indigenous governance, is relationships—with one another, the land, sea, ice, and all that live upon it. Borrowing from Leanne Simpson (2001), and as a matter of survival, research on and about Indigenous peoples must cease. Research governance is informed by Indigenous governance. These relationships, as noted by Indigenous scholars Wilson and Kovach, demand responsibility and accountability to all of one's relations. In the same way that Indigenous people are held accountable for their relations as a practice of good governance, so too are Indigenous peoples responsible and accountable for their relations in self-determined research.

SELF-DETERMINING A PATH IN COMMUNITY SUSTAINABILITY RESEARCH

The community governance and sustainability research which I (Hudson) led was guided by Indigenous and qualitative research methodology. While the former was used as the primary guide, aspects of the latter that support Indigenous research methods were also employed. Indigenous methodology that privileged the voice of NunatuKavut Inuit as local experts in their respective communities set the tone for this work, largely through interactive workshopping, gatherings, and community meetings which supported collaborative and consensus-building team discussions. Other more traditional qualitative interview practices and data collection strategies were employed (i.e., one-on-one interviews, focus groups, and surveys); however, the former methods were more successful in engaging and soliciting the expert knowledge and experience of NunatuKavut Inuit in this study.

Three pilot communities were chosen for the governance and sustainability research. These communities are remote (varying degrees of remoteness in NunatuKavut) and maintain a rich cultural heritage (deep connection to land, water, and ice). However, these communities have also experienced the loss of a major industry . The goal of the research project and the anticipated role of each community was explained vis-à-vis their relevant governing community council, and their interest in participating in this project was sought. Communities were contacted by email and telephone. All three communities eagerly agreed to participate. It is anticipated that lessons learned from work led by these pilot communities will also benefit other NunatuKavut communities.

Black Tickle, with a population of approximately 115, is the northernmost of the pilot communities. On an island off the southeast coast of Labrador, the community is a year-round fly in/out community with ferry service from June to November, pending ice conditions. With the cod moratorium of the 1990s and the closure of its fish plant in 2012, the community, once the site of a vigorous cod fishery, has been without a supporting industry. Yet, it maintains strong cultural connections to the land, sea, and ice and residents are eager to work toward a sustainable and vibrant future so that they can raise their children and grandchildren, while passing on knowledge and values that come with belonging to this wonderful place.

Norman Bay, south of Black Tickle, has approximately twenty people. Like Black Tickle, Norman Bay has no access to a highway; travel to/from the community is by helicopter or small boat. Reinvigorating a local economy, whereby residents do not leave their homes for seasonal employment, is paramount for most residents, along with transportation to/from the community. Like Black Tickle, Norman Bay has a rich cultural heritage and residents are eager to find sustainable solutions so that they can raise their children in the community, which continues to connect families to traditional knowledge and values.

St. Lewis, located south of Norman Bay, with fewer than 200 people, unlike Black Tickle and Norman Bay is connected to the TLH and maintains year-round airline service to the community (albeit, like Black Tickle, minimal airline access and costly). Like Black Tickle, St. Lewis's major industry was its fish plant, which closed in 2013. As such, the community is eager to identify opportunities for sustainability so that residents can remain in their homes, raise families, and share in tradition, history, and culture. St. Lewis, too, has a rich cultural heritage and remains connected to the land, sea, and ice.

Recruitment for the research relied heavily on community members and I (Hudson) took direction from the NCC to recruit potential participants in NunatuKavut pilot communities. Participants were recruited from the three pilot communities and others if individuals had left their ancestral community. Representatives from pilot communities (town mayors, local service district chairs, community

leaders, knowledge-holders, sustainability coordinators, etc.) identified other community leaders, knowledge-holders, and Elders who
were interested in participating in the research (either as interviewees
or as informants throughout various phases of the governance and
sustainability work during community workshops, meetings, gatherings, etc.). External partners and consultants, past and/or present,
were recruited to share their role in and knowledge of NunatuKavut's
journey as well as to reflect on and discuss NunatuKavut community
governance and sustainability from their experiences. Participants
were recruited individually and by public means, including verbally,
email, telephone, and public posters (i.e., in post office, stores, clinic,
etc.). Community participants were revered as "experts" relating to
matters impacting their home communities and the research topic. In
order for this research to be meaningful, direction and authority
came from community members themselves.

In keeping with Indigenous research methodology and in learning best practices in working with the pilot communities, other
forms of data collection included community gatherings and workshopping as well as capacity building in areas identified by residents
(i.e., proposal writing, asset mapping) and individual community
member submissions detailing what they love most about their community. These submissions further advanced understandings of
community and cultural values and priorities about conservation
and preservation of lands and resources. According to Wilson, "traditional Indigenous research emphasizes learning by watching and
doing" (2008, 40). This is why community engagement practices
(such as gatherings and capacity-building workshops) worked well
as a source of knowledge-sharing and -gathering, and ultimately,
data collection. Pre-existing research data and traditional knowledge
studies held by NCC also informed this study.

Finally, my own experiential knowledge (Hudson, as both community member and NCC research department lead), reflexive journaling, and relationships with and commitment to NunatuKavut communities, before and after this study, indicate an approach to research that is grounded in Indigenous ways of knowing.

Reclaiming and privileging Inuit knowledge and local community expertise was vital to the sustainability research in Black Tickle, Norman Bay, and St. Lewis. This research sought to facilitate opportunities for community members, leaders, youth, Elders, and knowledge-holders, to discuss and bring to life stories of what is most important to them and the future of their communities. An approach that acknowledged that Inuit are the experts in their communities allowed for community participation in sustainability research that was both motivating and empowering. This, I (Hudson) argue, worked in multidimensional ways—between communities and me as researcher and community member. Indeed, as an Indigenous researcher, I have learned invaluable lessons about the role of community in informing research on their/our lands.

The sustainability research used a strength-based approach which was groundbreaking in effectively engaging the pilot communities. Often, people become consumed with things that can and do go wrong and in what is not working well. This can be especially true in regions like NunatuKavut, where communities experience population decline and a loss of employment and other economic development opportunities through provincial and federal government cutbacks in programming and services. However, this research offered an opportunity and space for communities to envision a future that reflects who they are, their priorities, and their values. By doing so, communities identified short-, medium-, and long-term plans for sustainability. In many cases, they identified ways they could work together and/or learn from one another in building healthy and sustainable communities. Throughout this work, communities were active and self-determining participants in visioning a future that they could be proud of while re-connecting with their culture. Of importance to pilot communities was preserving and sustaining a connection to the land, sea, and ice. Community sustainability, or development, was considered sustainable only if it had minimal impact upon their cultural values, tradition, and way of life.

In my role (Hudson) as researcher and facilitator throughout the sustainability and governance research, I was reinvigorated by communities' interest in determining their potential and future direction. I was humbled by the wealth of cultural knowledge and the communities' expressed connection to place, as community members discussed self-determination, community governance, and sustainability. I learned quickly in this relationship that when you revere Inuit as experts, and facilitate opportunities for communities to engage in matters that are of stated importance to them, community involvement is successful. As a result of the sustainability research, the pilot communities identified priority sustainability areas and are partnering in diverse research projects to that end, some of which include food security and renewable energy research, both integral to community self-determination and -governance. Community expertise and knowledge, as it relates to the sustainability of these three communities, is essential to Inuit self-determination and to defining and setting the parameters of the research relationship on their lands and on their terms.

CONCLUSION

In linking colonial research practices to Indigenous peoples and communities, Smith explains:

It angers us when practices linked to the last century, and the centuries before that, are still employed to deny the validity of Indigenous peoples' claim to existence, to land and territories, to the right of self-determination, to the survival of our languages and forms of cultural knowledge, to our natural resources and systems for living within our environments. (2012, 1)

Smith's words carry deep meaning and she cites examples of colonial research practices that deny and invalidate Indigenous claims to existence and territory: they inform a history of research that has been perpetuated on Indigenous peoples the world over, and certainly, in NunatuKavut.

The ability of Indigenous peoples to self-determine in research is impacted by their ability to self-govern. When communities engage in research relationships that respect Indigenous autonomy, self-determination is evident. Opportunities for self-determination in research occur when research in Indigenous communities and by Indigenous peoples is informed by Indigenous knowledge and ways of being, all of which give rise to collective community priorities. Self-determined research is that which seeks to honour people, place, and culture throughout the research relationship and is governed and regulated by relationships (Cunsolo and Hudson 2018). In discussing research and Indigenous peoples, Smith asserts that "real power lies with those who design the tools" (2012, 40). In the case of NunatuKavut Inuit, who have been advancing research ethics since 2010, research is approached from the vantage point that communities are the experts in matters that impact them and their future (Bull and Hudson 2018; Cunsolo and Hudson 2018).

By building on the strengths of the participants in this research,

Inuit have identified pathways for self-determination in research that are grounded in their ways of knowing and being. As a result, they are better equipped to exert their autonomy and impact the future of their communities on their own terms. Both research governance work (to date) and community sustainability research have set a positive tone and increased expectations for community engagement and research participation in a way that honours and privileges local community knowledge and expertise. As it is for NunatuKavut Inuit, and for many Indigenous peoples, research is about survival (Smith 2012). It is about countering colonially embedded research relationships and impacts that have perpetuated intergenerational harm and trauma onto Indigenous peoples. While research is historically, and presently, often associated with colonially rooted power, Indigenous communities, such as those in NunatuKavut, are increasingly recognizing the power of anti-colonial research and its role in advancing self-determination and -governance efforts.

ACKNOWLEDGEMENTS

We thank the communities of Black Tickle, Norman Bay, and St. Lewis for their participation in this research and for expanding our knowledge base as it relates to doing research with and for community. Their knowledge, expertise, and commitment to home and community enlightened understandings of what it means to live sustainably. It is our hope that Inuit-led research will continue to create opportunities for community sustainability into the future. We thank the NCC for guidance and support throughout this journey and all journeys where Inuit self-determination is privileged and honoured.

REFERENCES

Brunger, F., and J. Bull. 2011. "Whose Agenda Is It? Regulating Health Research Ethics in Labrador." *Études/Inuit/Studies* 35, nos. 1–2: 127–42.

Brunger, F., and T. Russell. 2015. "Risk and Representation in Research Ethics: The NunatuKavut Experience." *Journal of Empirical Research on Human Research Ethics* 10, no. 4: 368–79. doi: 10.1177/1556264615599687.

Brunger, F., J. Bull, and D. Wall. 2015. "The NunatuKavut Model of Research Oversight: Innovation through Collaboration." In *Toolbox of Principles for Research in Indigenous Contexts: Ethics, Respect, Equity, Reciprocity, Cooperation and Culture*, edited by N. Gros-Louis McHugh, K. Gentelet, and S. Basile, 51–59. Wendake, QC: First Nations of Quebec and Labrador Health and Social Services Commission.

Brunger, F., J. Bull, and D. Wall. 2016. "'What Do They Really Mean by Partnerships?' Questioning the Unquestionable Good in Ethics Guidelines Promoting Community Engagement in Indigenous Health Research." *Qualitative Health Research* 26, no. 13: 1862–77.

Bull, J. 2010. "Research with Aboriginal Peoples: Authentic Relationships as a Precursor to Ethical Research." *The Journal of Empirical Research on Human Research Ethics* 5, no. 4: 13–22.

Bull, J. 2016. "A Two-Eyed Seeing Approach to Research Ethics Review: An Indigenous Perspective." In *The Ethics Rupture: Exploring Alternatives to Formal Research Ethics Review*, edited by W. C. Van den Hoonaard and A. Hamilton, 167–86. Toronto: University of Toronto Press.

Bull, Julie, and Amy Hudson. 2018. "Research Governance in NunatuKavut: Engagement, Expectations and Evolution." *International Journal of Circumpolar Health* 77: 1–4. doi: 10.1080/22423982.2018.1556558.

Corntassel, Jeff. 2008. "Toward Sustainable Self-Determination: Rethinking the Contemporary Indigenous-Rights Discourse." *Alternatives* 33: 105–32.

Corntassel, Jeff. 2012. "Re-envisioning Resurgence: Indigenous Pathways to Decolonization and Sustainable Self-Determination." *Decolonization: Indigeneity, Education and Society* 1, no. 1: 86–101.

Coulthard, Glen Sean. 2014. *Red Skin, White Masks: Rejecting the Colonial Politics of Recognition.* Minneapolis: University of Minnesota Press.

Cunsolo, Ashlee, and Amy Hudson. 2018. "Relationships, Resistance and Resurgence in Northern Led Research." *Northern Public Affairs* 6, no. 1: 23–28.

Inuit Tapiriit Kanatami (ITK). 2018. "National Inuit Strategy on Research." www.itk.ca.

Kovach, Margaret. 2009. *Indigenous Methodologies: Characteristics, Conversations, and Contexts.* Toronto: University of Toronto Press.

Leddy, Leanne C. 2018. "Historical Sources and the Beothuk: Questioning Settler Interpretations." In *Tracing Ochre: Changing Perspectives on the Beothuk*, edited by Fiona Polack, 199–219. Toronto: University of Toronto Press.

Martin, D. H. 2012. "Two-Eyed Seeing: A Framework for Understanding Indigenous and Non-Indigenous Approaches to Indigenous Health Research." *Canadian Journal of Nursing Research* 44, no. 2: 20–42.

Moore, Sylvia, Amy Hudson, and Erika Maxwell. 2018. Review of Nunatu-Kavut's Inuit Education Program. Internal Report to NCC.

Rigney, Lester-Irabinna. 1999. "Internationalization of an Indigenous Anti-colonial Cultural Critique of Research Methodologies: A Guide to Indigenist Research Methodology and Its Principles." *Wicazo Sa Review* 14, no. 2: 109–21.

Simpson, Leanne. 2001. "Aboriginal Peoples and Knowledge: Decolonizing Our Processes." *The Canadian Journal of Native Studies* 21, no. 1: 137–48.

Smith, Linda Tuhiwai. 2012. *Decolonizing Methodologies: Research and Indigenous Peoples.* 2nd ed. Otago, NZ: Otago University Press.

Stewart-Harawira, Makere. 2013. "Challenging Knowledge Capitalism: Indigenous Research in the 21st Century." *Socialist Studies* 9, no. 1: 39–51.

Wilson, Shawn. 2008. *Research Is Ceremony: Indigenous Research Methods.* Halifax: Fernwood Publishing.

Strengthening Inuit Self-Determination in Research: Perspectives from Inuit Nunangat

A Thematic Session and Discussion at the Inuit Studies Conference 2016*

Natan Obed, Scot Nickels, Ellen Avard, and Jennifer Parrott

INTRODUCTION†

(Natan Obed, Inuit Tapiriit Kanatami [ITK]. Moderator)

Research structures in Canada are not created to provide self-determination to Inuit, and they don't support the goals that we have for ourselves in research. It's really interesting to be a part of that world in a time of reconciliation and a time where people are more sympathetic to Inuit, more sympathetic to Indigenous people, because sympathy doesn't mean that the needle is going to be pushed toward self-determination. The self-interests of academic institutions and the self-interests of governments often come way before the interest in ensuring that self-determination happens for Indigenous peoples

---

*   Editor's note: This chapter was created from a transcript and a videotape of the event. It has been edited for readability, but we have tried to retain the sense of a partly informal group presentation and discussion. The session was formally introduced by David Lough, then deputy minister of Culture and Tourism, Nunatsiavut Government.

†   Editor's note: The first few seconds of this introduction were clipped from the videotape and the transcript.

in Canada, specifically Inuit. But we've done amazing things. I think what we're going to hear today is a cross-section of not only great best practices and emerging partnerships but also a sense of where we want to go from here. So, with that, I'll tell you about the format: we're going to have the presenters come up one at a time, they're going to speak for no more than ten minutes, and then we will bring everyone up at the end to have a question and answer dialogue with the room about the concepts that we have heard today. I invite each presenter to come up and either use the podium, to stand here, or, if you have a slideshow, to operate that. So without further ado I'll introduce Scot Nickels, who is the director of Inuit Qaujisarvingat, a department within Inuit Tapiriit Kanatami also known as the Inuit Knowledge Centre, and his department works with all of our regions on the big concepts of research and how we can work together across Canada to ensure that we do achieve self-determination.

INUIT SELF-DETERMINATION IN RESEARCH, A NATIONAL STRATEGY

Scot Nickels (Inuit Tapiriit Kanatami [ITK])

Thanks a lot, Natan. I wanted to start off with some of the work that we have been doing on research. I recently ran across a report from a 2001 research forum that I helped to organize. But in looking back at the report, it clearly outlined all the challenges and some solutions for research that we were discussing back then with academic, government, and Inuit researchers. It suddenly struck me that the things we were discussing back then, about sixteen years ago, are the same things that we are discussing and dealing with today: the same challenges, the same attempts to find solutions. Things like community research fatigue, the development of Inuit research priorities, giving value to Inuit knowledge, improving the way research relationships are built, issues of research consent, ethics, ownership, control and access and possession of information—these were things that were discussed at the 2001 research forum. These are things that we are still dealing with today. Lack of Inuit involvement, appropriate funding, and unrealistic timelines in research were things that were discussed at that forum that we are still talking about today. So, it just struck me: how much have we actually advanced over time? And we find Inuit still experience the reality that they have to fight just to get a seat at the table, and Inuit have to fight to become part of the governance structure of large research programs. The investments of money, of prestige, and of knowledge tend to accrue to the south rather than remaining in the north—and we need to find some solutions for this. We need some sort of foundational shift to get beyond where we are now, so that in ten to twenty years I'm not going back to a report that we are doing this year that is just saying the same things that we said back in 2001. Inuit self-determination in research is something real and something that we're going to have to move toward. The need to overcome colonization in research, and using all the tools that are at our disposal, is something that we're really eager to move forward on. And given that it's Thanksgiving weekend, I'll give thanks that we have some tools to move forward with, and I'll just point out ITK's Strategy and Action plan for 2016 to 2019, that provides me in my role at ITK, and in my role in working with regional organizations and representatives of those organizations, some marching orders to move forward with on the issue of Inuit self-determination. This document, if you go to look at it, there are seven objectives, and the sixth objective is Inuit self-determination in research. And one of the key deliverables of this document—the one that gives me and my staff marching orders—is the development of an Inuit research strategy.

And so we have begun to put measures in place to start the development of this Inuit-specific research strategy. In developing this, we will be working with our ITK board, which is made up of the presidents of each land claims organization and governments of Inuvialuit Settlement Region, Nunavut, Nunavik, and Nunatsiavut; we will be working with our Inuit Qaujisarvingat national committee, which has similar representation as the ITK board of directors, and this committee will be able to provide recommendations and advice up to the board. We will be working with the Inuit Circumpolar Council of Canada, with the Inuit Women's Organization Pauktuutit, and with the National Inuit Youth Council. And of course Inuit won't be doing this in isolation: we'll be working with academic and government researchers as well to ensure that we have their inclusion and their expertise; but really the focus here is for Inuit to move forward, developing an Inuit research strategy on Inuit timelines and with Inuit methodologies, and working with other researchers that are interested in working with Inuit. So we are just flipping things over in the way they tend to run typically. Some of the things that we'll be looking at in developing our Inuit research strategies are some of the things I've already talked about: developing Inuit-specific priorities, regionally and nationally; Inuit-specific methodologies for research to counterbalance some of the methodological discrimination that still occurs out there; dealing with researcher roles, training, and things like accreditation for Inuit within research; approaches to reduce research fatigue in Inuit communities; issues of research ethics, ownership, control, access of information; things like interoperability and standardization across the arctic; issues of informed consent; and of course methods for safeguarding the rights of Inuit in research. We are also exploring, in an evening meeting here at this conference, an Inuit-specific data advisory committee to bring Inuit together to coordinate issues across regions that pertain to data management and information discovery, and so forth.

So, in conclusion, because I'd like to leave a lot of time for our other speakers, Inuit have been by and large subsidizing a lot of Arctic research activities with their time and effort. Inuit are the ones that will pay the price when things go wrong in Arctic research. So we feel strongly that it's time for Inuit to define their own research priorities, to lead their own research projects, and ultimately to develop and control their own research policies, their narratives, and the individuals and people that they work with, not in isolation, but meaningfully connected to others who are doing research. I think the Inuit research strategy, as it's being developed, will provide a tool, and the beginning of a solution toward improved Inuit self-determination in research. So I think I'll leave it there and move on to the next speaker. Thanks.

THE NUNAVIK RESEARCH CENTRE: SINCE 1978 ...

Ellen Avard (Makivik Corporation)
Thanks everybody, thanks Dave, thanks Natan, and a special shout-out to Scot for bringing us all together here this morning. I'm going to try to go through really quickly, under ten minutes, and give you a brief introduction to our research centre. Nunavik Research Centre, since 1978—it was created following the signing of the James Bay and Northern Quebec Agreement in 1975. This is something that I find very extraordinary: Inuit of Nunavik created their own research centre to respond to questions and concerns that they have, so it's a pretty great example across the circumpolar North. We're located in Kuujjuaq and we've got eight full-time staff, more than 50 per cent of whom are local Inuit from Kuujjuaq. Aside from me—I'm a relatively

new addition to the team since 2009, and I've been full time for two years now—we've got Barrie Ford, who many of you know, a wildlife biologist and deputy director; our toxicologist Michael Kwan, who's been there almost twenty years now; our fisheries biologist, Lillian, who came the same time as I did around two years ago; three wildlife technicians—these guys have been here between twenty-five and thirty-five years, so they've been here since the beginning—-Peter May, Sandy Suppa, and Alix Gordon; Susan Nulukie, our secretary, who has been with us for a couple of years now, and this is really great because Susan not only does secretarial work, she also gets in the field with us and works in the lab. So many of these guys have been here for decades now, and what's really interesting is they have a lot of substantial corporate history and knowledge.

So this [*slide*] shows the Nunavik Research Centre (NRC): its head office, our research warehouse, and boat shed. The mandate is to promote and conduct research based on concerns, questions, and objectives of Nunavimmiut; to promote and mentor interests and in-volvement of Nunavimmiut in scientific research. We try to do as best we can in terms of youth outreach, both youth from the north and youth from the south, because people from the south don't know about the north—I didn't know about the north until I started to come to work there, so it's really important that we do this cross-pollination between northerners and southerners. We respect and incorporate traditional Inuit values and knowledge when conduct-ing research and promote collaboration with the NRC, universities, and government, because we can't do it all by ourselves.

I'm just going to give you a quick overview. I sort of cherry-picked five projects just to give you a quick idea: our fishway study, the beluga population studies we work on, some walrus work, some analysis in metals and contaminants, and a little bit of wildlife aging.

First, our fishway project. Originally the Nepihjee watershed was inaccessible to migrating Arctic char due to a set of falls. In 1998, in collaboration with Nayumivik Landholding Corporation, a fishway was blasted into the rock, and a hatchery was put together to put fish directly into the water system. Allan Gordon, who many of you know, received a very prestigious award for his work on this, and the ultimate goal was to provide the community with a sustainable Arctic char fishery. Not only was the base work done, but we also continue monitoring this every year; and here is where we pull in a lot of local students, so of course this creates youth employment opportunities, and transfers a lot of valuable knowledge and skills in scientific sampling and assessment techniques.

Now, our beluga study. Many of you are involved in this work. The way it goes is that at the centre we prepare kits, we send these kits up to the communities and local community coordinators, and hunters are able to get these kits and take them out hunting with them. When they're done, they package samples and send them in to us. We take care of all the logistics. We do some of the analysis in our lab, then what we can't do at home we send out to different government labs. We also have a new beluga program started last year, a biopsy program, where we're looking at addressing sustainability, at addressing questions and trying to find answers about the eastern Hudson Bay beluga whales. Here again we're working very closely with local hunters. What's interesting about this program is that we can obtain samples without killing whales, so we're able to work with those folks in charge who establish the quotas, and still able to get the data. We have a whole team of local hunters from different communities who come into our lab for training, and we do what we can in our lab and what we can't do, we work with the Department of Fisheries and Oceans Canada. The goal is to define the annual movement of the

Hudson Bay beluga, and of course this data will go up the line to improve management and conservation positions regarding harvesting.

Next, our Trichinella program. Many of you probably saw last week a beautiful article in *Nunatsiaq News* where four young kids from Iqaluit killed their first walruses, and on the bottom it says that once the meat has been sent in for testing and it's safe to eat, it will be distributed into the community. Well, those four walrus tongues came to our lab to test the meat, and it was Sandy and Peter who tested those walrus tongues. It was nice to see that on *Nunatsiaq News*, front and centre. Trichinella is a parasite found in walrus and polar bear meat, and it can lead to serious illness if the contaminated meat is not cooked. The walruses are tagged once they've been killed, and then a piece of the tongue comes into our lab and we analyze it. Our researchers are even working this Thanksgiving weekend: there were six walrus hunted just a few days ago. So they don't take time off; they get results back within twenty-four hours to communities in Nunavik, and as soon as possible—usually within a couple of days— to communities within eastern Nunavut. So [*slide*] here's just a quick overview of the lab process, and once were done, and we have results, they are sent to the Director of Public Health and then communicated to the mayors.

We also have metal analysis facilities, and we were the first Aboriginal organization in the Canadian north to establish these types of facilities, so we do a lot of work on contaminants. Our lab was founded in 1997, so almost twenty years ago now, and we are on par with all the best labs in the country, and that's really something that we are quite proud of. So Nunavimmiut can test for contaminants in country food without having to rely on outside help. And in the same spirit as our other programs, we return the results back to the communities in a timely manner and usually in conjunction with advice from the health board. We also are building an in-house database of country foods, both animals and plants, and with this we are able to do monitoring of long-term trends.

As just a quick example of a contaminants and metal analysis project: the objectives of the Lake Trout Project were to collect data to assess how much lake trout contributes to total dietary mercury intake, and also to see if there was a consistent relationship between fish age, length, and weight, and the amount of mercury accumulation. In this past year there were 150 fish collected from five villages, with the assistance of community members, and here once again we rely on really strong partnerships with folks in all the villages. This 2015 study was a repeat of a 2006 study, so all in all, with the two studies, we have 490 samples from over nine villages in Nunavik. Once again, we talk about data collection and community partnership, and I think we're really doing some good things here. The analysis work is conducted at the Nunavik Research Centre in Kuujjuaq, and these findings are going to help health authorities develop recommendations for the consumption of lake trout, and it's with a special focus on pregnant women and women of childbearing age.

Finally, a quick overview of a last example: wildlife aging. Many of us often have questions about the age of the wildlife that is hunted, and there are a lot of different techniques for different species—beluga, fish, mussels, scallops, and caribou. Peter Mays is our specialist in this, and we will get requests from across the country for Peter to work on other data that has been collected elsewhere. Here [*series of slides*] is Peter working on beluga teeth, and this is what it looks like; there's salmon scales, and some lake trout. In this case we're looking for ages for our own internal projects, as well as to help out folks from the Quebec Ministere des Foret, de la Faune et des Parcs, and the Department of Fisheries and Oceans Canada, for example.

So just to close up—hopefully I haven't been too fast—all projects are examples of longstanding Inuit-led conservation initiatives, community capacity building, education, and northern cultural values. So *nakurmiimarialuk*, thanks very much everybody.

[Natan Obed (Moderator)] To touch very briefly on the work we do at the national level, different land claim agreements have different provisions that are very helpful. The James Bay-Northern Quebec Agreement has specific sections in relation to housing that allow for Nunavik to have a more robust housing program that's directly linked with its land claim than other jurisdictions. Article 32 in the Nunavut Land Claims Agreement [NLCA] is something that isn't a shared provision in all of the Canadian Inuit land claim agreements, so the right to participate, and in such a broad way, especially in consideration with the federal government, is something that I think is one of the most powerful provisions in the land claim agreement, but also one that is the least understood. And also one that I would imagine is going to take litigation and a lot of dialogue over the next generation to come to a place in which not only Inuit in Nunavut can benefit from what comes out of those discussions, but all Inuit in Canada. Next, I'd like to call on Jenn Parrott, who is with the Inuvialuit Regional Corporation.

SELF-DETERMINATION IN RESEARCH

Jennifer Parrott (Inuvialuit Regional Corporation [IRC])

Good morning everyone. My name is Jennifer Parrott, and I work for the Inuvialuit Regional Corporation. Established in 1984, the IRC has been entrusted with implementing the Inuvialuit Final Agreement, which is associated with the western Arctic. Today I'm going to be providing you with an overview of how the Inuvialuit Final Agreement is associated with research activities in the western Arctic, then I am going to go through how research itself has changed in the western Arctic, as well as a bit about Inuvialuit involvement in the research licencing process. Lastly, I'm going to provide some of our annual research priorities and talk about how these priorities can be integrated into research itself.

The Inuvialuit Settlement Region is located within Canada between the northwestern side of Nunavut and northeastern Alaska. It has a 91,000-square-kilometre area, including 19,000 square kilometres of privately owned lands. The region was officially recognized in 1984 with the signing of the Inuvialuit Final Agreement, and what's important with this Final Agreement is that it ensures that there are Inuvialuit interests and voicing around both renewable and non-renewable resources, as well as research. As in the presentation prior to mine, there's a clear linkage between the Final Agreement signed in this region, and research itself.

The Inuvialuit Final Agreement, or IFA, sets out three clear principles. The first principle is to protect and preserve Arctic wildlife, environment, and biological productivity. The way to do that, set out in section 14, subsection 1, is through the application of conservation principles and practices. In order to do that we need adequate information, and what is laid out in subsection 5 is that the relevant knowledge and experience needs to come from both Inuvialuit and scientific communities. So the Agreement ensures that there is a collective partnership between the Inuvialuit voice and the research community, be that academic or the federal or territorial government. In order to have that adequate information, subsection 80 states that it is adequate research that will produce the information that can then be used for management and conservation purposes. It reads, "Comprehensive and continuous research and scientific investigation are required in the ISR to provide information on which decisions affecting wildlife and the environment can be based. Whenever possible, studies should be undertaken by existing public and private institutions"—whether those be the Inuvialuit bodies themselves, federal or territorial governments, academic institutions, or sometimes the private sector. To ensure that this is done in an equitable manner, there is a clear linkage to the research advisory council in subsection 84. Now this advisory council is designated to collect and collate the existing data, identify research gaps, commission special studies, and recommend future research. It's important to note here there's a majority of seats of Inuvialuit representation on this advisory council, it's chaired by the Inuvialuit Regional Corporation, and it has partnerships with the federal and territorial governments. So what we can clearly see from an analysis of our Final Agreement is that there is a very clear linkage between Inuvialuit voice and research that's conducted in our region. So on paper it should be very easy to have self-determination in research. In the past we haven't always seen that as the case, which is too bad.

As a component of this, now that we accept the importance of having an Inuvialuit voice in research itself, we're going to look at the research licencing process to see how the Inuvialuit bodies are incorporated in this process. In the event that you are interested in doing research in the western Arctic, whether you're academic, federal government, or territorial government, there's a three-step process that occurs. The first stage is the local process, to make direct engagement with local Inuvialuit organizations. Now, for the federal government this looks very different than for many of the academics that are sitting in the room. The federal government is, I guess, determining the priorities for how research is carried out, and also determining exactly which projects receive funding, and the Inuvialuit voice has to be at the table to ensure that those funds are set out properly. And through an annual research review cycle there are Inuvialuit bodies that sit at that table. For academic researchers, there is a bit of a gap here: we don't have that clear linkage where we have an annual process, we have individuals sitting on boards, and there is a clear presentation and review of research. Academics are kind of set out on their own to navigate this system, which can be quite confusing at times. I guess it's important to note that while the local and territorial stages can be done in conjunction, it's not really recommended because local support is required for territorial licence, which is very different from some of the other regions. The Inuvialuit Regional Corporation, or any of the co-management boards that are appropriate to your research, need to sign off on it for you to receive a research licence in our region. So, very different: if you're not doing that initial communication piece, you may stumble around that second stage. The territorial licence is done through the Aurora Research Institute [ARI], and this is research licencing as per the NWT Research Act, and this will also give you all of your permits around the wildlife act, handling of species, and contact with human subjects, and those sorts of things. The only reason here where we touch on the issues is that we'll see applications come through the research licencing process, and we'll have no idea who these people are, and there won't be a linkage between Inuvialuit-driven priorities and the research that's being proposed. And once all that is said and done, we're on to the last stage, the regional stage. There are two additional pieces. One is an environmental impact screening review, so that in the event your research is going to conduct any harm to the environment, Inuvialuit bodies have their own co-management system that does an assessment of this. And lastly there's an application for access to our private lands. In order for a researcher to cross over private lands and conduct research, it is, I think, an $80 processing fee; but we need to know who's coming into the region, where they are, how long they're there for, and to ensure all the appropriate licences have been acquired. So that's your last step. And although you might think, "Holy smokes, this is a huge amount of time and effort. What the heck's going on here?" And while we know you researchers have your funders to contend with, and all this other stuff, please note that much of this can be done in a very short period of time, as long as there's clear communication and understanding of what you want to do, and what needs to be done.

So within the Inuvialuit Settlement Region [ISR] there's already an established system for setting up Inuvialuit priorities. Those priorities are set by the Inuvialuit Regional Corporation in communication with community members, hunters and trappers associations, the regional community councils, as well as any other respected co-management board. As an example, the Fisheries Joint Management Committee does fish and marine mammals; we also have wildlife councils, environment councils, and those sorts of things.

Here is a quick overview of our priorities that have been set for 2016. First is the exploration and acquisition of knowledge and information to improve social, cultural, and economic conditions. This seems very broad, and it's broad on purpose so as to invite specific projects that other individuals may have to bring into the region, to see how they can benefit our communities. The second priority is to promote sustainable development and increase local capacity. Here there is a focus on ensuring that Inuvialuit individuals are being hired with research teams, and that there's knowledge transfer right from the collection of data, all the way to the delivery of information at the end. There has been quite a history in many of the Arctic regions where researchers come up, bring their own research assistants, do their own work, leave, mail up a poster, and call it a day. That system has changed a bit in the western Arctic over the last few decades, and we want to continue to see a more solid integration between the academic community, the federal public service, and Inuvialuit bodies. The third priority is wildlife monitoring of key species, and the key species for 2016 are caribou, beaver, beluga, and char. There are already existing research programs that address each of these. Fourth, there's a revitalized focus on community-based monitoring as the form of research that is most heavily favoured in our communities. We'd like to see that continue moving forward. The next priority is a focus on climate change and shipping activity, with the new cruise ships that get the exciting opportunity to see the western Arctic for the first time. We had two ships come here this year: huge, huge ships—pretty neat stuff. The last priority is looking at storm surges and coastal erosion. Our region has a massive amount of coastal erosion, and we need to have a better understanding of what's going on there.

The other important thing that's been a change is that Inuvialuit were seen as research subjects in the twentieth century, but now that we're moving forward we're seeing Inuvialuit as researchers themselves, as advocates for researchers, and full collaborators in the research process. And in the past, as I've mentioned, primary research projects were really to the primary benefit of the researcher. Even up until recently we saw a real focus on funding agencies, especially in the academic community: "A funder is willing to give me funding for this, therefore I'm going to impose that on your community," in order to promote an individual's career, or carry on in the academic landscape. But we're seeing that change a lot in the western Arctic, because by setting our research priorities so early on in the fiscal year, it's easy for researchers to tune in and also stay aware of being engaged with Inuvialuit bodies. As our research priorities change, you can see what's coming next to determine your funding applications accordingly. And as research opportunities continue to grow in the ISR, self-determination becomes increasingly important to ensure that there's mutually beneficial research occurring, and that it's occurring with equal partnership. As well, we're seeing a shift toward evidence-based decision making, and the integration of science and traditional knowledge in our region. An example of that is with the community conversations that have been developed, through the Inuvialuit Game Council, the Fisheries Joint Management Committee, and the Inuvialuit Regional Corporation. We're seeing that even Inuvialuit bodies are starting to take in more science and more academic-focused information, and incorporating that with traditional knowledge; and we'd like to see that continue to happen in the academic community as well.

Overall, research is a central focus and an important decision-making tool in the ISR, and it's important to have all organizations that are established under the IFA, as well as federal partners and academia, work together to ensure that the future in the western arctic is a successful one and a sustainable one. Thank you.

[Natan Obed (Moderator)] I want to add a couple of points. One is that the current Inuvialuit Regional Corporation CEO and Chair, Duane Smith, is one of the biggest proponents of the sustainable national health survey; and at the recent ITK AGM, we as the Inuit representational leaders across Inuit Nunangat said that we're going to move forward as quickly as possible to ensure that we have a sustainable Inuit health survey. The other point is in relation to the protocols that you went through, I can recall when we did social and cultural reviews for International Polar Year projects—that seems

like a long time ago now—it was a step forward at the time in that Indigenous people could actually sit on social and cultural review committee. We couldn't make determinations for the entire project, but we could give advice to the scientific review panels. And there was one application I can remember that came in, and when it came to adjudicating the community involvement of the proposal, the response from the researcher was, "I tried, I don't know how, but I'm willing to do whatever you tell me," and that has been the attitude for a long time: just throwing your hands up and saying, "Well, you're the expert in that, you know what to do." Whereas, I think within self-determination, in the way that we want to go, it's "No, you have an obligation, and we are telling you that you need to do this." It isn't up to the community to take the interpretation from the researcher: it is up to the researcher to come to the community and discuss what it means, in partnership. So the protocols that you're putting in place in the Inuvialuit region are exactly the ones that I think should be in place across the country.

If I could get the rest of the panelists to come, take a seat. And now I'd like to open up the room for questions of our panelists. Please, when you are asking your question, I will ask you to use your outside voice and also to identify the person you're wanting to ask the question to, or if it is a question to the entirety of the panel. Thanks.

Question 1, for Inuit Tapiriit Kanatami (ITK)

Questioner: You had your list of objectives for the research priorities, and you went through some of the things you're going to be tackling, and one of the things I didn't hear on that list was around funding. I know in various projects and things that we've tried to get funding for together, to try and forward some of the causes you mentioned, that one of the big issues is around eligibility for Tri-council funding of Inuit organizations. ITK in some cases having to go through a process every single time you want to apply, as opposed to being qualified in advance like a university would be. Is that something that maybe is on the list but didn't get mentioned? Or could you maybe put it on the list? Because I think ITK has a role to play there.

Scot Nickels: Without a doubt it's a huge issue. For years we've been going through institutional eligibility through the Tri-council to have Inuit-led research, and even still we are having to, and obligated to, use research ethics boards of certain academic institutions. We have a lot of hoops to jump through in the application process, and we don't always see ourselves in it—it's really geared for academic institutions. In terms of being successful and getting funds to do that, we found ourselves hampered by review committees that don't understand arctic research, and that's something we have to work on to change.

Natan Obed: I can jump in there as well. We do talk about this issue every day with the federal government, and also with bodies like the Canadian Institutes of Health Research (CIHR), trying to reimagine our place within their structures: whether we are actually on governing committees, or within processes in relation to funding, or basic organizational capacity and the eligibility for that. Just to give you an example of some of things we've had to do in the interim, through the National Inuit Committee on Health we wanted to partner with ITK to put a layer on top of the CIHR call for Pathways, which was suicide prevention, tuberculosis, and a couple of other health priority areas that they had identified themselves, without Inuit even being involved in it. What we basically did was call for any researchers who were going to apply to Pathways to first apply to ITK. ITK would then, through the National Inuit Committee on Health, vet those proposals, and then choose to partner with particular researchers for that specific call. How that played out was that one of the partners that we chose to endorse got a letter back from CIHR saying they weren't successful, and part of the reason why they weren't successful is that they didn't show they had a true partnership with Inuit. And that is where we are: they didn't even understand at CIHR the importance that our endorsement played in having that researcher put their proposal forward, and what that meant for Inuit involvement. That's how far apart our worlds are at this time.

Question 2, for Inuvialuit Regional Corporation (IRC)

Questioner: Just recognizing the different governance structures within each Inuit region, and the different implementation and land claims processes across Inuit Nunangat. I was probably a bit more curious to understand a little bit more from NWT on the structure and relationship between IRC and the Aurora Research Institute [ARI], because I believe that's where the licencing goes. I'd just like to know a little bit more about the thought process, because that seems to be also a similarity, I believe, to Nunavut.

Jennifer Parrott: Before we answer that question, I want to welcome John Noksana Junior, who's sitting with me today. He's also associated with the Inuvialuit Settlement Region: he's sat on many co-management boards to determine research priorities, and who receives research. So thank you for sitting with me at the panel to help answer questions. The relationship between the ARI and the Inuvialuit Regional Corporation (IRC): IRC sits as the Indigenous body that governs the area known as the Inuvialuit Settlement Region and ARI is not directly associated with us in terms of the implementation of that Inuvialuit Final Agreement [IFA]. The Aurora Research Institute has a partnership with IRC, and through that partnership ARI has understood the importance of having an Inuvialuit voice that determines what type of research is happening in the region. Through that partnership we have a direct window into every person who applies for a licence, the review period that's required by us to review each licence and provide comment, and also determine if we provide an endorsement to issue a licence or not. In the event we don't issue endorsement, ARI does not then issue the licence, and a continued conversation occurs between ARI, the academic institution, or federal or territory public service, as well as the associated co-management group, be it IRC or any of our wildlife management groups. So there isn't anything formal around the IFA that creates that partnership; it's through a partnership that's developed over time why we have that clear linkage.

Questioner: And how does that work?

Jennifer Parrot: Oh, it's great! Today—not talking about tomorrow or five hours from now—but today that relationship is one that's respectful. As someone who gets to see every application that goes in, our commenting field, and to see the way that research is carried out, for us right now the primary concern is ensuring that Inuvialuit are hired to help collect the information, help analyze the information, and deliver back in the communities; to help ensure that as research is continuing to get huge in our region nowadays, that information isn't just collected and taken away, there's an issue there. There's also an issue around the appropriate delivery of information, because IRC is capable of taking and hosting all the data that was collected; and we have our own archives, cataloguing system, and database; so ensuring that researchers are aware of that and deliver the data back to us for our individual management decisions.

Question 3, for Inuit Tapiriit Kanatami (ITK)

Questioner: I've heard some discussion around the development of a research guideline for Inuit Nunangat, and we've heard some great examples from each region. If ITK were to develop a research ethics guideline for Inuit, and, although the process is similar in the four regions, there are some differences—different priorities, different ideas of how to do it—how is it going to be set up? Is it going to be one big ethics guideline for Inuit Nunangat, or is it going to be separate for each region? Thinking about Nunavut, there are three regions there, different priorities there again. How is that feedback, that dialogue, going to happen within your organizations, within the regions of Inuit Nunangat, to ensure it's getting what people are saying they want, and it's getting what, you know, a large portion of Inuit are saying? It's going to be a big process, and I'm just curious as to how that dialogue is going to happen, because there's, you know, community-based projects going on, there's regional-based projects going on, territorial-based and Inuit Nunangat-wide. It's huge: how are you guys going to do that?

Scot Nickels: Thank you very much for your question. That's a great question. I think the closest we have to something like this is the Relationships Bulletin, a very general document on how to create research relationships with Inuit. And that's a dated document, and things that are in that are already dated, so something needs to happen in terms of a guideline. But you're talking about something even more than that, and there have been discussions that followed from our involvement in the Tri-council policy statement review. The Tri-council policy statement review is to look at Inuit-specific research ethics guidelines, and even the establishment of an Inuit-specific research ethics board. And you're right, those are huge issues. I think the opportunity we have to address those issues and how to go about it, a beginning of those conversations would be in our development of the Inuit Research Strategy, and having discussions with our regional representatives, organizations, and governments; to have discussions to figure out how that will all unfold and in what direction it is best to head. So you're right, those are issues that are on the table for discussion; there's been interest in moving forward on those things, and I guess we'll have opportunities to create that path of what will work out best. I'd open that up to anybody else.

Natan Obed: To add on that, if you are looking at the people who are going to try to make that happen, the limitations, and also the opportunities, that we have at the national or federal level are very different then the regional or community levels. And just as in any other major policy discussions, what we can leverage at the national level and can then translate into action or funding or improved relationships at the regional and community levels, often starts with really solid work at the national level to ensure that those things can happen. So we at the national level know our role, and our role isn't to change research priority area at the community levels, it's to ensure that the research agenda across Inuit Nunangat has a solid foundation. Anyone else want to comment?

Question 4 (partly inaudible), for all panelists

Questioner: Experiences with co-management are starting to really narrow the definitions of IQ (Inuit Qaujimajatuqangit) or TK (Traditional Knowledge) or IK (Indigenous Knowledge). I just wanted to ask, is there a feeling across your organizations that the acceptance of Indigenous Knowledge is shrinking?

Jennifer Parrott: I can start. In the Inuvialuit Settlement Region, when we look at how research has changed over the region, I would say it's the opposite, I would say that right now traditional knowledge is considered as valuable or more valuable than a lot of the scientific work that's being done. It's awesome to be at a place to be able to say that now, and it's from years and decades of fighting to say "What are you doing?" Individuals in the communities know what's going on right now, and whether you have a microscope or if you have a recorder, you could've saved yourself a lot of money and time. I think that relationship is being better understood in the western Arctic now, so I would say that it's the opposite, for our particular region.

John Noksana Junior: I think as an academic or scientist, if you come and know nothing about the region, or whatever, you're better off going to the people and saying, "How would you propose we do this?" It could save you time, effort, and money. The better information you have, the better the outcome at the end of the day. And that's the whole point: to get the right information. So you have to listen to the people at the local levels: how to do things, when to do things— stuff like that.

Natan Obed: I just would add that some of this fight perhaps is at the federal level, or the national level, where the idea, and even the way that you characterize our knowledge—whether it's science, or whether it's traditional, all of these different competing terms that have all sorts of qualifications to scientific knowledge as the academic community understands it to be—that's where I think a lot of our efforts are going to be. I think researchers that are coming to the communities, coming to our regions now, understand the importance, and that is partly the reason they are interested. Good question.

Question 5, Anybody

Questioner: This is a quick comment, and kind of a question to consider. It's about monitoring. I worked for the Nunavut Water Board over the summer and we looked at a lot of applications that concern research, and monitoring specifically, and the terms and conditions for monitoring. It seems that monitoring fulfills a very western scientific standard. Monitoring through monitoring stations, or in labs, will tell you about a lot of things, but it won't necessarily tell you how the kinds of environmental impacts are affecting Inuit. This seems to imply that research is done for the purpose of satisfying western scientific standards, and I was wondering if any of your organizations would consider using traditional Inuit monitors, which might involve Inuit going out on the land, going hunting and recording back on their experience. It's great that you guys are training Inuit to work within this scientific monitoring system, but it would be nice to value Inuit for the knowledge that they do have, that they can provide.

Natan Obed (Moderator)

I appreciate your comment, and I think there'll be further conversation. I'm sure each one of our panelists could have an in-depth conversation about that.

I'd like to thank all of our panelists for their presentations. Thank you!

Notes on Contributors

Christopher Alcantara, professor of Political Science at the University of Western Ontario, has written five books, including *Nested Federalism and Inuit Self-Governance in the Canadian Arctic*, with Gary Wilson and Thierry Rodon (UBC Press, 2020).

Ellen Avard is the director of the Nunavik Research Centre, Makivik Corporation.

Julie Bull heads an independent consulting business that helps to identify and implement emerging, promising, and wise practices in research ethics and engagement with Indigenous Peoples. She is also an adjunct professor in the Division of Community Health and Humanities in the Faculty of Medicine at Memorial University.

Tom Gordon is a professor emeritus at Memorial University's School of Music. Since 2003 he has collaborated with Labrador Inuit in documenting social practices and cultural expression.

Amy Hudson, from the NunatuKavut community of Black Tickle, is a PhD candidate at Memorial University with a research focus on Inuit governance and community sustainability. She is the Director of Research, Education and Culture at NunatuKavut Community

Council and negotiator on its Recognition of Indigenous Rights and Self-Determination team.

Beverly Hunter, who lives in Hopedale, Nunatsiavut, is a former counsellor for the Trauma and Addictions Mobile Treatment team with the Nunatsiavut Government; she currently works as an Elder's Coordinator.

David Lough began working in Labrador in 1972 and has been involved in community and economic development throughout the region. From 2010 to 2016, he was deputy minister of Culture, Recreation and Tourism with the Nunatsiavut Government. He co-chaired the 2016 Inuit Studies Conference.

Scot Nickels was, at the time of the conference, Director of Inuit Qaujisarvingat, the Inuit-specific research centre at Inuit Tapiriit Kanatami. He has since left ITK.

Natan Obed is a native of Nain, Nunatsiavut. At the time of the conference, he was the recently elected president of the Inuit Tapiriit Kanatami. Since then he has been returned for a second term as leader of Canada's national Inuit organization.

Maatalii Aneraq Okalik is from Panniqtuuq, Nunavut. From 2015 to 2017 she was president of the Inuit National Youth Council, a senior policy advisor for the Government of Nunavut, and a student in Human Rights and Political Science at Carleton University.

Jennifer Parrott was, at the time of her original contribution, the Research Manager for the Inuvialuit Regional Corporation. She is currently the Director of Innovation, Science and Climage Change for the Inuvialuit Regional Corporation.

Andrea Procter, an anthropologist with almost twenty years' experience in working with Indigenous communities in Labrador, coordinated the *Daughters of Mikak* initiative with an advisory group of women from across Nunatsiavut.

Lisa Rankin is a professor of Archaeology and Research Chair of Northern Indigenous Archaeology in the Department of Archaeology at Memorial University. Since 2001 she has conducted research in Labrador in collaboration with Inuit communities.

Bruce Uviluq is a negotiator with the Legal Services Division at Nunavut Tunngavik Inc.

Graham White, Professor Emeritus of Political Science at the University of Toronto, has been visiting and writing about the Canadian north since the 1980s. His most recent book is *Indigenous Empowerment through Co-Management: Land Claims Boards, Wildlife Management and Environmental Regulation* (UBC Press, 2020).

Charlotte Wolfrey has sat on regional, provincial, national, and international committees, including Pauktuutit Inuit Women of Canada and the Provincial Advisory Council on the Status of Women. She served for many years on the Rigolet Inuit Community Government and the Labrador Inuit Association and is currently the AngajukKâk (mayor) for Rigolet.